MY DAYS WITH
ALBERT SCHWEITZER

MY DAYS WITH ALBERT SCHWEITZER

A Lambaréné Landscape

Illustrated by the Author

FREDERICK FRANCK

LYONS AND BURFORD, PUBLISHERS

To the Grand Docteur and to my little son, Lukas

Printed in the United States of America

10 9 8 7 6 5 4 3 2 1

Library of Congress Cataloging-in-Publication Data

Franck, Frederick, 1909–
    Days with Albert Schweitzer : a Lambaréné landscape /
Frederick Franck ; illustrated by the author.
        p.   cm.
    Originally published: New York : Holt, 1959.
    ISBN 1-55821-195-0
    1. Schweitzer, Albert, 1875–1965.   2. Missionaries,
Medical—Gabon—Lambaréné (Moyen Ogooué)—
Biography.   I. Title.
R722.32.S35F73   1992
610'.92—dc20
[B]   92-13975
                                                                CIP

Acknowledgments

Especially profound thanks to MEDICO (Medical International Corporation), a division of the International Rescue Committee, of which Dr. Schweitzer is Honorary Patron. It was MEDICO which supplied all the equipment for the clinic, took care of my transportation, and honored me on my return by appointing me to its Executive Committee, thereby allowing me to participate further in its world-wide mission of mercy: bringing medical help from America to areas where all medical help is lacking. I also wish to thank MEDICO for giving me what may be a last glance at an Africa which still looked peaceful and unchanging.

I should like to thank my friends Franz Schoenberner, who read and edited the manuscript, and B. J. Chute, whose keen and sensitive judgment encouraged me.

I am grateful to my friend Dr. Herbert M. Phillips, president and founder of the Albert Schweitzer Education Foundation, who performed dental work at Lambaréné Hospital long before I did and who contributed valuable preliminary information.

My thanks are extended also to Pfizer Laboratories, Division Charles Pfizer & Co., Inc., for its generous permission to use four drawings from its collection and to the following for making drawings in their collections available: the editors of *What's New* (Abbott Laboratories), the Museum of Modern Art, Mr. Lawrence Gussman, Dr. Paul Benacerraf, Mr. Leo Cherne, Mr. John Richardson, Mr. Ben Wechsler, and others.

Without the help of Claske Berndes, who assisted me in Lambaréné and not only typed the manuscript but collaborated on it throughout, the book could never have been written.

F. F.

Contents

Illustrations

Introduction to the 1992 Edition

I was in a small town in central France in 1965 when my eyes fell on the newspaper headline in heavy type, "SCHWEITZER MORT". I grabbed the paper and read the flowery eulogy. It was replete with all the clichés common to the usual, sentimental Schweitzer rhapsodies. I remembered once reading such an account to him when it appeared in an Italian magazine. He shook his head and grunted, "Believe it or not, but that Schweitzer is coming out of my ears."

His response was typical of his terse sense of humor and hardly fit the solemn Schweitzer myth that had crystallized around him during his long life. The Schweitzer myth, however, must be neither shrugged off nor underestimated, for it is one of the very few positive, life-affirming myths of humanness and goodness born in this appalling century. His was indeed a mythical story, in the true sense of *myth* as a poetic narrative that points to the mystery of life and its meaning.

Here was the extraordinarily gifted son of a small-town Lutheran pastor who had developed his immense potentialities to their utmost limit—as a revolutionary theologian, as a profound yet practical philosopher, and as a great organist and musicologist who by the age of

thirty had written a definitive study of Johann Sebastian
Bach. Then, suddenly, he gave up an uncommon multi-
plicity of brilliant careers, resigned from his professorate
at the University of Strasbourg, and decided to study
medicine. This decision came about after reading a plea
from the Paris Mission Society for help in Equatorial
Africa, where the people were in desperate need of a
medical service that was totally lacking. Becoming a doctor, he reflected, would enable him to "work without
having to talk. For years now I have been giving of myself
in words, but in this new commitment, I'll not be a talker
about the 'Religion of Love', but one who puts it into
practice."

Schweitzer gained notoriety as the unorthodox author
of "The Quest for the Historical Jesus" (1910) which
shocked both liberal and conservative Protestants. None-
theless, its concept of a 'Religion of Love' laid the foundation for the exceptional medical missionary he was to
become. As the price for cooperation from the Paris Mission Society, Schweitzer had to accept its condition that
he would neither preach nor officiate. In my understanding, this was precisely in line with Schweitzer's inten-
tion. He became the atypical missionary who, in his fifty
years of medical practice in the jungle, did not convert a
single one of the "heathens" he took care of day and
night. He simply wanted to be a living witness to the
'Religion of Love,' render a limitless service of love and
compassion in the spirit of its founder, and be a Christic
presence, rather than a denominational "Christian," in
the heart of darkness and human suffering.

Driving through France on that day of mourning in
1965, I felt overwhelmed when I realized my extraordi-

nary privilege of having worked alongside this towering figure—not the hero of a myth, but an immensely *human* being—allowed to sit opposite him every day at a table, and to talk with him. These conversations, most of them about practical matters and daily chores, were conducted in that courteous style inseparable from him, as natural as it was contagious. Ever more clearly I came to see Albert Schweitzer not as the saint he never pretended to be, but all the more as a pioneer, even a prophet.

I stopped my car on the shoulder of the Route Nationale and jotted down what, in the next quarter century, would confirm itself abundantly:

• Albert Schweitzer pioneered a human future in the face of an ever worsening dehumanization of our species.

• He was a pioneer in foreign aid, but of a kind to which no political strings were attached. It required neither secretariats, nor bureaucracies, nor public relations agents. The necessary funds were raised for years through Schweitzer's organ recitals all over Europe. It was the kind of foreign aid where one put himself on the line—mind, body, and soul.

• He was a pioneer in missionary work that did not consist of sermonizing and was not measured by the number of converts made. It was *mission* as a total commitment to the alleviation of suffering.

• He was a pioneer in ecumenism. He radiated respect for anyone's religious conviction and never even inquired about a person's religious affiliation or non-affiliation. "Dogma divides, the Spirit unites," I once heard him say, dismissing some visitor's attempt at theological hairsplitting. He said grace before meals, but it was such that only a dogmatic atheist could not join in.

- He was deep in his eighties when, in 1957, he pioneered once more with a protest against nuclear testing. Schweitzer was the first person in his position of prominence to do so forcefully, eloquently, and with his usual directness and courage.

- Schweitzer's principle of "Reverence for Life" is nothing, if not a matter of life and death for humanity in our violent age. He put this indispensable principle into practice for half a century, and it is needed *now* more than ever, at this time of suicidal contempt for life manifest in the annual condemnation to death of fifteen million children by starvation, neglect, and malnutrition; in the death verdict to our rain forests, to thousands of animal species, and to the ozone shield which is vital for life on earth as we know it; and in the billions of dollars spent every day to produce more weapons for mass murder, shamelessly exported to whomever is prepared to pay for them.

  "Reverence for Life" is the standard by which national policies, technologies, and corporations should be judged as being either compatible with, or antagonistic to the humane criteria that have sustained viable civilizations throughout history. These criteria can only be disregarded at the price of the extinction not only of our civilization but of our species.

- It must not be forgotten that Albert Schweitzer, born in 1875, was a pioneer in ecology long before the word entered the vernacular. He revered and protected the forest environment of the hospital he built in 1913 instead of bulldozing it. Nothing was wasted in Lambaréné and hardly anything was imported for our table. The plentiful fruits and vegetables we ate were grown in the wonderful gardens he created. He wrote his "Philosophy of Civilization" on the back of flyers, envelopes, bills—any of the scraps of paper he gathered on hooks above his writing table. On one of those scraps he prophesied, "All our advances in knowledge and power will prove fatal to us in the end unless we regain control over them by a corresponding advance in our spirituality."

Schweitzer's spirituality was the opposite of that wishy-washy sentimentality that often passes for it. Neither was it a watertight compartment separated from his daily life and work. It was totally integrated in the *uncommon* sense with which he faced everyday reality—a perspective of *ultimate reality* for want of a better term.

His "Reverence for Life" was the very opposite of an indulgence in sentimentality. It was grounded in a constant awareness of the mystery of life, which made it unthinkable for him to ever inflict pain on any living thing gratuitously, thoughtlessly, and without feeling, or to sacrifice even a worm's or a rat's life without conscientiously weighing its inevitability.

He was more than a pioneer, a prophet of what we now call ecology. Rachel Carson dedicated her epoch-making *Silent Spring* (1960) to Schweitzer, quoting him: "Man has lost the capacity to foresee and forestall. He will end by destroying the earth." In his acceptance speech for the Nobel Peace Prize in 1954, the jungle doctor diagnosed the malignancy of nationalism as one of the worst scourges of our time. He had seen it manifest itself during both world wars, as we now see its lethal metastases spreading over the five continents.

Albert Schweitzer's life and its message have never been more urgent than they are now, at the threshold of the twenty-first century. I am grateful to my publishers for making this new edition of the simple story of *My Days with Albert Schweitzer* once more available. I dedicate this new edition not only to the memory of this paradigm of human greatness, but to all who toil to keep Albert Schweitzer's presence alive today when it is more crucial than ever—

The Albert Schweitzer Institute for the Humanities, P.0. Box 308, Wallingford, Connecticut 06492

The Albert Schweitzer Fellowship, 866 United Nations Plaza, New York, New York 10017

The Albert Schweitzer Center, RD #1, Box 7, Great Barrington, Massachusetts 01230

Maison Albert Schweitzer, Gunzbach, France

and to my wife Claske, who not only assisted me in Lambaréné but without whom this book, the ones that followed it, and life itself are unthinkable.

—Frederick Franck
June 1992

MY DAYS WITH
ALBERT SCHWEITZER

Prologue

I was working in my practice on a May day of 1957 when my nurse told me that Mrs. Clara Urquhart wanted to talk to me on the telephone. The nurse is not supposed to disturb me and when she does, it means that someone of unusual authority insists.

Clara told me that she had just arrived from Lambaréné, which is not surprising for she is always arriving, if she is not leaving, for somewhere, and that somewhere is quite often Dr. Schweitzer's Hospital. When we met that evening she said, "Here you sit in New York making a fat living. If you only knew how they need dental help in Lambaréné."

She had hardly finished her sentence before my mind was made up. "When shall I go?" I asked my old friend Clara.

She thought I was joking, so I repeated my question very seriously and added one condition: "I'll set up a clinic and work as hard as I can a good number of hours each day and the rest of the day I'll draw and write. That's what I do here too."

Correspondence with Dr. Schweitzer followed and less than a year later I left.

It was not to be my first contact with Dr. Schweitzer; as a boy, when he was still quite unknown in America, he was one of my idols. When I was studying medicine and dentistry in Edinburgh, Scotland, in 1936, Schweitzer gave his series of Gifford Lectures there and I was one of his faithful listeners. And when in 1949 he returned to Africa from his participation at the Aspen, Colorado, Goethe Bi-Centennial, I happened to be on the same boat.

Many things attracted me to Lambaréné. And they are all explainable by my past. After studying medicine in my native Holland and obtaining degrees in dental surgery in Belgium and Scotland I settled in London. I built up a rather fashionable practice which did not completely satisfy me. Hence I soon started to do voluntary work for various needy groups like the Basque refugee children who came to England during the Spanish Civil War. Afterward I did similar work for Mennonite refugees from Hitler-Germany and finally joined a group of Quaker relief workers who brought help to a then "distressed area" in a mining district of South Wales.

I had always been most interested in the arts and it was actually only parental force which drove me away from pen and brush and toward scalpel and forceps. But the older I got, the stronger the original impulse became. I began to paint and draw seriously and professionally and used my medico-dental equipment as an economic life buoy which kept me pleasantly floating and gave me freedom to do whatever I wanted in the arts.

After I came to America and had to study once again, I settled down to a split but regulated life in which art and dental practice kept an antagonistic balance.

If you split your week between a busy practice and much drawing, painting, and writing, it is difficult to do voluntary dental work as well.

When Clara mentioned the need at Dr. Schweitzer's Hospital I saw in a flash that here Providence in the pleasant shape of Clara Urquhart offered me for the first time in my life a chance to do something in which my drawing, my dental surgery, and my writing would not conflict with one another, but on the contrary could be integrated at last.

And so I flew to Lambaréné and this book is one of the results. Before I went, I read a good part of the extensive literature on the subject, often overflowing with milk and honey. Therefore, my picture of Dr. Schweitzer and his Hospital proved, like that of most people, to be a false one.

There is in Lambaréné an ancient man

Much Nonsense and
Some Sense

*I*t is high time that someone should publish an authoritative, definitive condensation of all the nonsense written about Albert Schweitzer and Lambaréné.

The mythical Albert Schweitzer does not exist. There is in Lambaréné an ancient man, still with the body of a giant, sitting at his table writing or digesting clippings from the world press, supervising every detail in the functioning of his Hospital.

Contrary to so many misleading reports, the Hospital is not situated in an eternally steaming jungle. Innumerable black bearers are not at one's beck and call, and I

4

didn't see a lion or a leopard during my entire stay. In three months I saw only one tiny scorpion, neatly put outside in a towel. By special dispensation I met one snake and had to drive about forty miles in order to see, not an elephant, but a few unmistakable souvenirs left by this majestic animal after too laxative a meal. Reality does not seem to matter to the hundreds of scribes who pen their adventures in or about Lambaréné. I often wondered how many of these literati have really been there. The staff told me that indeed a high percentage of them have spent an afternoon or so in Lambaréné. If accompanied by his wife, the writer usually stayed in his room and sent the Missus around the Hospital with a camera and a notebook while he began to type. The wife, also straight from New York or Copenhagen, had never seen an African village in her life. Well smeared with insect-repellents, she was promptly horrified by the squalor in which the poor patients are housed, the huge tropical ulcers which seem a specialty here but in fact are a scourge all over Africa, the unappetizing native cooking behind the sick wards. She is disgusted by goats, chickens, and cats roaming through wards and consultation rooms . . . or she just *loves* the primitiveness of it all, raves about the native cuisine, boasts about the rugged life in Lambaréné, gushes over the loving, head-stroking nurses, the good doctor worrying at the bedside of every single patient, his leonine head in his hand, or philosophizing under a pineapple tree. Little does it matter that pineapples don't grow on trees but prosaically like squashes on the ground.

Native cooking behind the sick wards

The account is apt to give descriptions of Dr. Schweitzer taking his morning swim in the river, playing toccatas on the famous piano-organ before breakfast, and holding forth about Reverence for Life. Afterward, he will be photographed supervising the amputation of a leg crushed by a gorilla. At lunch he will prove that he is a reactionary tyrant ruling over his little empire with an iron hand; hymns will be sung and Bible reading follow.

Who cares that hymns are never sung after lunch and that Dr. Schweitzer reads from his Bible after dinner? Don't the article-spouting visitors have to catch a plane in the afternoon? Can't one telescope his experiences a bit?

For our picture of Lambaréné, let's start with the Ogowe River as a swimming hole: the water is contaminated by a most unpleasant parasite called bilharzia, which penetrates the skin and causes a serious, hard-to-treat disease. Natives indeed wash in the river and children frolic in it. The result is infection. All over Africa bilharzia is a nearly invincible problem.

Schweitzer frowns on his staff using the all too unstable pirogues. Not because he is afraid of frisky hippos or playful crocodiles, not because he fears that his nurses will drown when their tiny craft is upset, but simply because contact with the water is dangerous.

The morning swim sounds like a British contribution of Schweitzer apocrypha. A French twist is best illustrated by the following incident. Returning from Lambaréné I stopped at my favorite small hotel in Paris. I had hardly put down my bags when the *patronne* started questioning me, wiping her hands with her black apron in excitement: *"Eh bien, docteur,* is it true that Dr. Schweitzer is living with a rich young American petroleum heiress?"* The hymns after lunch were invented by a devout Scandinavian pastor, the plumbing hardships are usually broadcast by all American visitors, and the picture of a soulful Bismarck whose fluorescent *"Dichter und Denker"* eyes roam the nocturnal Ogowe are a German creation.

After recording all this nonsense, something has to be said about the glib diagnoses of Schweitzer's attitude toward the "blacks." The devotees maintain that he loves them indiscriminately like pets, interminably stroking their woolly hair. According to professional debunkers he rules over them with a whip and lashes them when they contradict him: an "old-fashioned colonialist," a "reactionary" who denies their basic humanity and simply uses them as tools for his megalomania. Both views are equally hysterical. His attitude toward native Africans is necessarily complex. After all, he has lived here during the last forty-five years, a crucial period in which revolutionary changes have taken place in the world in general but in Africa and Asia in particular.

Just as I was leaving Africa these changes were gaining momentum and a few months later even the name "French Equatorial Africa" already was obsolete. The virus of nationalism has penetrated the African organism completely, pitting black against white and often black against black.

After some months of intimate contact with the Africans of the Gabon region, what had first looked like a homogeneous mass dissolved into a myriad of personalities. What had first looked like a solid block of black physiognomy became atomized into hundreds of faces of three or four ethnic types, each greatly different from another and all separated by deep abysses of antipathy.

I found myself completely detached from these antipathies and saw individual people; each one of the hundreds of faces is engraved separately on my consciousness. Notwithstanding cultural differences I found myself in close human contact with many whose names are already becoming vague, but whose faces and personalities have enriched me permanently. I was fortunate in being able to speak French with them, for nearly all the Gabonese people speak some French which they learn in school. Often the contact was more direct and profound with those who were still "primitive" than with those who had adopted white man's customs. The former seemed to have more innate dignity and were more open than those who with their wrist watches, brief cases, camera cases, and window-glass spectacles tried to imitate our most unpleasing aspects. The half-evolved people who use these symbols in their despair are as hard to take as half-educated Westerners who need similar crutches. Similar inner conflicts make mutual understanding difficult. Their inferiority feelings, expressed in distrust, insecurity, and insincerity, make it impossible to establish anything resembling the intuitive, immediate rapport which comes naturally with people who have not reached this stage in an unbalanced and perhaps illusory westernization. I remember many Africans, mostly in their forties and fifties, who had not absorbed superficialties, but who had developed a mellowness and a delicacy of feeling which one rarely meets in whites.

What touched me immediately about the Africans of the region? The ease with which I established communication with them. Not just linguistically, but humanly I felt immediately a natural contact. I found them extremely sensitive to mood and approach and marveled at the lack of destructiveness in their lovable and bright children. Immense potentialities are here to be nourished, starved, or perverted.

My personal experiences gave me insight into the complexity of Schweitzer's feelings in the matter of race relations. I saw a similar complexity in an old and noble Jesuit missionary who for thirty-eight years had worked in a particularly primitive part of the Belgian Congo:

he too loved his tribes with all his heart, he too was disturbed by the superficial "evolution" of haphazardly chosen individuals, uprooted and lost, belonging nowhere, discontented and arrogant.

Father d'Espierres expressed it well: "We missed our chance. We destroyed their original social structure and gave them nothing instead. We half-educated some of their children, we neglected to raise the level of family and clan life, we disrupted everything. We did it all with our heads and all too little with our hearts."

For some people it may be easy after a two-day visit to make superficial judgment of Schweitzer's attitudes and call them colonialist or reactionary. After a few months of intensive work and experience with the Gabonese, and especially of drawing them—there is no more intensive way of looking—I would not judge. I did not come to Lambaréné to reach any dogmatic conclusions. I came to experience, to absorb, and, above all, to work.

The Road
to Lambaréné

Lambaréné is scarcely more difficult to reach than most other points on earth. You can, as Dr. Schweitzer still does, take a slow boat from Bordeaux, stopping at all the African ports along the coast until you get to Port-Gentil from which a small motorboat will take you in a few days to Lambaréné. Or you can fly. I flew from New York to Leopoldville in a flying tin can with reclining seats, ate the unavoidable chicken à la king from aluminum dishes and was grinned at periodically by standardized hostesses. All I like about air travel is to feel, after ten or twelve hours of pseudo-normalcy, some solid concrete under my feet!—even such a short break as we had in Nigeria on a small airstrip with a camel or two standing around to add local color.

At Leopoldville, a little dazed because of all the tranquilizers, I was driven to a hotel, a hotel like any other, air-conditioned and all. Immediately I was warned by every well-meaning soul not to give large tips to the innumerable black houseboys and spoil local labor relations!

The mysterious ways of airline companies make it necessary to have one airport at Leopoldville and one just as big about two miles farther in Brazzaville. The two cities, one the capital of the Belgian Congo, the other of French Equatorial Africa, are separated only by the Congo River and connected by ferryboats.

The Congo is a majestic stream, several times as wide as the Hudson, and looks a bit like a shifting meadow or, rather, a floating bulb field. The French accuse the Belgians and the Belgians accuse—according to political whim—either American, British, or German missionaries of having introduced the water hyacinths, beautiful plants with luxuriant greenery and fantastically luscious purple flowers, which thrived so well on Congo water that they spread like rabbits in Australia. Looking at the Congo River from my airplane I saw innumerable small green and purple islands move swiftly down the stream to the Stanley Rapids just below Brazza and Leo (the "ville" in the names of both towns is strictly for greenhorns). These rapids are formidable, an immense roaring maelstrom against which ill-fated ferries or motorboats are often rammed to smithereens.

The water hyacinths, imported into Africa only ten

years ago, have become an expensive problem, for they sometimes bring shipping to a standstill. This most decorative plague is now being tackled with chemical spray from airplanes and even with dynamite. But it is an unforgettable sight, well worth tons of dynamite, to see this river of flowers moving toward the sunset.

Since the airplane for Lambaréné belongs to Air France I had to leave from Brazzaville. Before boarding the ferry, one has to pass through customs. Hundreds of Africans, the men mostly in shirt and trousers, the women in colorful wraps, their children on their backs, Moslem traders from the Sudan in flowing woolen robes, steadily push one another past customs. Red-fezzed colored gendarmes keep the stream running smoothly, while custom

Red-fezzed gendarmes

officers go through a pretense of checking what is hidden between child and mother and among the indescribably complex loads which are momentarily lifted from heads. The Moslems go through it all with the debonair gestures of men-about-town which gave me the impression that under their burnooses were never-to-be-discovered treasures of ivory, gold, and secret documents. The small ferryboats have no color bar. However, there are two classes and the difference in fare acts as a segregation device. Only very elegant Africans with gold-rimmed glasses and brief cases were sitting on the upper deck.

At Brazza, the customs were more arbitrary, for one is now in *la douce France*. Stamps are slammed on any and all papers you happen to present and you have the impression that all of them are going to be checked by officious uniformed men every day of your stay. But of course nobody ever looks at them again.

The most shocking discovery at Brazza is that the French colonial franc is twice as expensive as the ordinary French franc and the luxurious motel kept there by Air France is prohibitive. But it has a chef who probably spends his vacations in Paris doing postgraduate work. He and the exquisitely furnished, spacious, and cool rooms, stainless steel bathrooms, and wide dining terraces overlooking the Congo River, plus the consciousness that it was to be the last luxury for months, made me forgive the bill.

Early next morning, I boarded the milk-run which officially has four stops before Lambaréné. Here all pretense at luxurious "normal" air travel stopped. The plane was an old one. The small passenger compartment was filled with black mamas, Moslems, a few fat colonials in shorts, a nun in white, and an emaciated bearded missionary reading his breviary. The steward was a very polite African, but with nothing to offer except warm beer or lemonade near the boiling point.

In the middle of the fuselage the plane was divided by a partition with a door that either stuck or flew open every minute. Behind it were the smelly foodstuffs which are delivered weekly along the route, along with machinery, tools, agricultural implements, and luggage.

The crew supervise the fueling, cigarettes in their mouths as though gasoline here were non-inflammable!

No blue unfathomable tropical skies. This was the dry season, when a thick blanket of clouds covers the whole region under a humid quilt. As the plane roared away it seemed that it would never again emerge from the clouds. The first scheduled stop proved impossible: ceiling too low. At my question whether there was radar aboard, the steward looked at me as though I had asked whether we were equipped with a symphony orchestra. At the second stop we seemed to land: flaps in, flaps out. But we didn't. The steward, very apologetically as though it were his fault, whispered, "Impossible." The plane gained height again. At the third stop: same story. The next landing was to be Lambaréné.

At last there was a hole in the clouds, the jungle became visible, and we really landed. "So here we are," I sighed.

Indeed we were, but not at Lambaréné. The pilot, on a hunch or a radio message that there was a hole in the clouds over stop number one, had simply turned back to deliver the *bifteck*. When finally we approached Lambaréné, the clouds looked more like a sieve with patches of too lush green visible through it.

Landing at Lambaréné is unforgettable. The plane swept over it, but there seemed to be no land, only clusters of tropical foliage bathed in innumerable arms of river, swamp, and lake. To land here appeared to be utterly impossible.

No landing strip was visible as the pilot skimmed over impenetrable masses of vegetation and water. Jungle seemed to propel itself toward the plane. I thought of a plane which some years ago had crashed on one of these hops, I think between Douala and Port-Gentil. Although they are not very far apart, it took two years before the wreckage was discovered. The clusters of green became larger and seemed like crystallization points of life in a world in formation.

Then, suddenly, there was the rough bump of landing gear on airstrip. As though it were the most natural thing in the world, a Germanic looking girl in a sun helmet was waiting with a wounded antelope in her arms.

"Hello," she said casually, "I am sorry I can't help you with your luggage, but I just found this poor thing with a broken leg. I guess someone at the Hospital can set it."

The African Air France representative in a braided cap threw the luggage into a trailer, we climbed into a jeep, bumped for a mile or so, and there was the Ogowe River, smooth and wide. On the opposite bank I saw the village of Lambaréné—some low houses, a few huts, and a large hotel.

As we approach the hospital

A pirogue, or dugout, was waiting with four or five oarsmen, and I, with my luggage, was transferred from the jeep into the unstable craft. Slowly the oarsmen started to paddle upstream.

After a while they began to sing—a polyphonous song which maintained the rhythm in the heavy upstream paddling. The singing became louder as we approached the Hospital, to signal that visitors were arriving. The bells of the Hospital started ringing. By the time the pirogue swung around the last bend of the Ogowe and the Hospital buildings became visible, a dense crowd had gathered on the beach. As we came nearer I saw white figures standing patiently at the landing, waiting.

Suddenly I was out of the pirogue and stood face to

A kind old man

face with the Legend himself. The Legend vanished within a second. There was a kind old man, but appearing not nearly so old as at eighty-four he might, with smiling eyes and a hearty handshake.

"Welcome," he said. "We have been waiting for you and I am glad you are here."

I felt welcome and that they had been waiting for me.

Life in Lambaréné

$\mathcal{A}$wakening next morning in a monastic little room in the Hospital I lay staring at whitewashed plank walls and a white sheet which served as a curtain for the mosquito screening which formed my window.

The bed squeaked as I turned around. It was a narrow army cot, not uncomfortable, just too musical. On the table near the window were two kerosene lamps: one with a green cardboard shade over its glass bowl was the reading lamp; the other, a safety lamp for use at night to walk around the Hospital grounds, for there is no street lighting.

Actually, the room was not really monastic at all; it

My monastic little room

was cozy, more like one I had once had in a little peasant inn in Austria. There, too, I had hung my rucksack on a nail and had fallen exhaustedly on a virginally clean, squeaky iron bed. . . . I poured water from the big pitcher on the floor into the enamel washbasin and washed, rinsing my mouth with boiled water from an old wine bottle. Looking for my shoes, I stumbled over that humble piece of sanitary equipment, the nearly forgotten chamber pot.

On all the enamel utensils the letters A.S.B., Albert Schweitzer-Bresslau (Bresslau was the late Mrs. Schweitzer's maiden name), have been painted. I have heard criticism of this ostentatious monogramming of all household utensils at the Hospital. The sensibilities of tough international reporters have been offended by this sign of vile suspicion. At least one of them professed horror at the habit of locking the door on leaving one's room. "Isn't it revolting," the shocked journalist exclaimed, "this attitude in a place so devoted to brotherly love?" It may be revolting, but it is perfectly sound, because actually people here are so desperately poor that any small enamel dish is a piece of working capital. Is it necessary to tempt them by flaunting all our unreachable luxuries in their faces—our watches, lighters, ballpoints, cameras, cigarettes, lotions, and costume jewelry? Don't these shocked idealists lock their hotel rooms on going out and their cars on parking in their own home towns?

That first day I opened my curtain and had my first early morning impression of the Hospital landscape, a practice which I was to follow daily during my stay. Between the tall trunks of the palms lies the grassy hill which, sloping down toward the Ogowe River, that vast sheet of luminosity, stretches out toward a horizon seamed with the darker green of dense vegetation.

Breakfast starts at seven-thirty, but you can come in any time before eight-thirty. It is the only meal which one eats at his convenience. Lunch and dinner begin with everyone present, except those detained by essential duties. It does not immediately strike the casual visitor that life at the Hospital is regulated by a long-established community routine. You could call it a secular monastic organization with Dr. Schweitzer as the abbot, secular because there is a wide range of religious belief and complete respect for religious freedom. The only religious ritual in which everybody on the white staff actively or passively participates is at the communal meals. At the beginning of each meal Dr. Schweitzer says a simple prayer: "Thank the Lord for He is kind and His mercy is everlasting. Amen." After supper he reads a short passage from the Bible and a hymn is sung. There is never a trace of emotional pietism or sentimentality about this. It is more as if a hallowed tradition is being continued instead of broken. When there are French-speaking guests the customary German is abandoned and the prayer and Bible reading take place in French.

Since life on this peculiar island in the forest has to be regulated in some way or other, the community organization bears the imprint of its founder in every detail. "I hate comfort," he once said to me. And so the Hospital never became a luxury hotel.

In the dining room Dr. Schweitzer's old piano stands against the wall between the huge windows. The long table is set by African houseboys. Large gray and blue water pitchers of heavy earthenware are placed decoratively in a row between the plates. There are perhaps twenty-five or thirty beautiful European peasant chairs which have been copied in Africa by Schweitzer's old carpenter. The table linen is always spotless and at night, after the table had been set and the oil lamps lighted, I often sat in the dining room alone and enjoyed its atmosphere of dignity and quiet.

The dinner music of the African evening made by cicadas and bullfrogs, which floats into the room, seems to emphasize the silence. After the gongs have been struck

The long table is set

rhythmically and many times, the doctors and nurses slowly enter. From the windows you see only the kerosene lamps moving through the darkness. Everyone places his burning lamp in the little hall, just as at lunch everyone puts his sun helmet there before entering.

When all are gathered, Schweitzer appears. He usually works in his room up to the last minute, but sometimes he takes a few minutes off to sit on the steps of his porch, watching the evening with one of the nurses, a few animals at his feet. The old man is perhaps most moving when he is sitting on those steps: very old, very tired, and yet expressing intense joy in being alive, content with his homestead wrested from the jungle and delighting in all of nature around him.

In early morning when he stands on the porch, before the cheap little mirror hanging against one of the supports of the roof, shaving with his old-fashioned razor, he gives that same impression of oneness with his surroundings. Occasionally, he will stop and look out over his yard with an expression of "good to be here" or perhaps talk a bit to one of his goats.

As soon as he enters the dining room he goes straight to his chair, which is midway of the long table. He sits down and while everyone else is still trying to find the place indicated by his special napkin case, Schweitzer has already folded his hands. The second the last chair has stopped scraping on the concrete floor he starts his short prayer. Immediately afterward conversation and eating begin.

Schweitzer's seat is the only one which never changes. The nurse who has been with him longest, Mathilde Kottmann, practically always sits on his left. Ali Silver, second in seniority, usually sits at his right, but she may move down one seat if protocol demands it. Who exactly is Chef du Protocol never became clear, but he or she functions as noiselessly and tactfully as any small Court could desire. There are usually guests from all over the world, but an important guest is always placed opposite the Grand Docteur and his two oldest assistants, which facilitates conversation. Other guests are distributed along the long side of the table opposite Dr. Schweitzer, and everybody else is shifted around to make space. Sometimes there are so many people compressed at table that passing the large dishes of food becomes a juggler's act.

Even this passing along is a ritual: one passes food from the center to the end of the table on both sides and nothing is to cross this hallowed frontier. In the beginning I committed many breaches of etiquette and was kindly but emphatically corrected. Of the various misdemeanors, the most serious are to serve the lady next to you instead of letting her serve herself, or to ask your neighbor politely if he would not like another piece of crocodile—if he wishes it he should ask you to pass it. To get up to introduce yourself to some guest coming a little late and being plunked next to you is also an infraction.

Conversation flows freely and the lower echelons at the ends try to shout to the upper ones closer to the center. I was fortunate in usually sitting practically opposite Schweitzer. He enjoys his food and often gets some extra little tidbits. Cooking is a complicated task here, for there are always some people with dysentery or other tropical disturbances who need special diets.

Cooking is a complicated task

Dr. Schweitzer looks at his extra piece of fresh pineapple, his nice fillet of carp with obvious pleasure. But before he starts eating, you may see him quickly glance around from under his heavy eyebrows. Someone who seems particularly deserving or perhaps particularly hungry is going to be favored. He shoves half of his pineapple or his fish toward the lucky one and says, "Here, that is for you." It is a fatherly command not to be contradicted. Once when I was all finished, he remembered that I was very fond of lentil soup. I got half his bowl, honestly shared. I am indeed very fond of lentil soup and I highly appreciated his attention, yet it cost me a little effort to eat it after my fruit salad. But he gives it with such sweetness that you would not dream of refusing it. I ate my dessert of lentil soup, beaming my delight.

Lambaréné is not a three-star restaurant, but the cuisine is good and abundant. This sounds simple, but it is hard to achieve. Tropical Africa is poor in many foodstuffs to which white people are accustomed. The better situated French are supplied by the weekly plane with their *escargots* and vegetables from Europe, but Schweitzer has tried to live as much as possible off the land.

The vegetable gardens, one of the minor miracles he performed on the equator, abound with luscious vegetables. Every meal starts with huge dishes of papayas, grapefruit, or other native fruits. Vegetables are well cooked under the supervision of a Swiss girl, Emmy. She is tall and strong with the noble features you see on nineteenth-century statuary—a Marianne raising her stone flag on a French city square or, come to think of it, our

The vegetable gardens

own Statue of Liberty holding up her torch. But here she brandishes the saucepan, beats the gong for dinner, and in these roles you could make a cast of her and have another fine statue to put at a harbor entrance.

Yet all the inventiveness of Emmy does not balance the diet. What is lacking is protein. Meat is rarely served; the local fish, usually carp, consists mostly of skin and bones. Sometimes an excellent large *capitaine*, similar to our snapper, is brought in, or a crocodile of which we whites eat only the tail. It tastes a little like a pork chop and I imagine a good French chef could make a series of masterpieces out of it. Crocodile cooked in the German manner is a little sauerbraten-ish or Wiener schnitzel-ish. It is hard to forget that you are eating a crocodile who would no doubt have preferred it the other way around.

Bread is baked on the premises from imported flour. On Sundays it is cakelike and particularly good. Butter has to be imported from Europe and is available at only three meals a week, unless somebody has a birthday. On birthdays, Sunday bread is eaten thick with butter.

Table conversation usually is lively, especially when Schweitzer, who is a gifted raconteur, tells about some occurrence from his rich experience. He always speaks to a particular person, never to an audience. He may ask one of the doctors about a patient who worries him, but he does not expect anyone to go into technical details during meals. If there are many guests and he suddenly decides that he has talked enough, he withdraws completely into himself. His hands, which still do not show a trace of tremor, will all at once start drumming on the tablecloth and you feel he is thinking music and his hands are running through a toccata or fugue. After supper, the moment the table has been cleared, the conversation dies down. Schweitzer has already looked through his hymnal and his Bible. When he announces the number of the hymn to be sung, you hear an old minister's voice. He has a particular churchy tone for this, which he never uses otherwise. Hymn books are distributed, he gets up heavily and goes to the piano. Then he starts improvising his prelude to the evening's choice. Often the same hymn is sung, but he never plays the same prelude. The style seems to depend on his mood. Sometimes he improvises in eighteenth-century style. The next evening his prelude may be classical or even romantic. His improvisations have reminded me of Schumann, Mendelssohn, or Beethoven, but they never are Schumann, Mendelssohn, or

Beethoven—they have always passed through Schweitzer.

The piano must be decades old, decades of tropical humidity. It is completely out of tune even by equatorial standards, but this does not disturb Dr. Schweitzer. He is attached to it as he is attached to all the objects which have accompanied him through his life. He is not a modern man who will discard things as mere things. They seem to have become beings to him, beings he started to love long ago and which become ever dearer as time goes on. What does it matter that certain keys of this piano are stuck and that no one else can play it at all? He knows which keys have died and his improvisation neatly circumvents them. What does it matter that some benefactor sends a new piano which is standing in a corner? It is all right for the nurses to play on. He remains married to his old one.

After the prelude we all sing together. This is a ritual too. Hardly anyone present would ever think of hymn singing were it not for Schweitzer, just as no one would think of demonstratively not singing as long as he is here.

After the hymnals are closed and he has slowly walked back to his chair, he'll start reading a chapter from the Bible. He does it in an even, matter-of-fact voice and after the chapter is read, he turns the pages to the Lord's Prayer and reads this just as soberly.

The commentary which follows is always interesting, but it is never meant for mere uplift. Again he speaks to one particular person at a time and what he says is based on his enormous knowledge, not only of theology but especially of the history of Christianity. He places the section just read, for instance from the Book of Revelations, in its precise historical context: "What is meant by Babylon?" Answer: "The Roman Empire."

After reading from the Epistle to the Hebrews where Christ is described as the High Priest and compared to Melchizedek, he will refer back to Genesis to show who this Melchizedek was.

If there is anything specifically "religious" about his commentary it is that he always stresses the fundamental value of religious experience which to Schweitzer is so much more important than dogma. "Dogmas divide denominations, but the spirit unites them. There are Catholics who have the spirit as well as Protestants. We Protestants can split up in as many sects as we may wish; it does not matter as long as the spirit is alive. That is all that counts." He uses the German word *Frommigkeit* when speaking of this essential ingredient. But I feel it should not be translated as "piety" but somehow as the act of experiencing life religiously.

He often reads from some unknown piece of early Christian literature to further clarify the historical context of the passage discussed. Usually the cuckoo clock in the corner interrupts his lecture long before it is finished. He glances at it, goes on a little longer, then stops. He firmly puts his hand on the table, is quiet for a second, and while getting up says, "Fine, and now back to work!"

He walks out, his lamp in his hand, usually Miss Kottmann at his side. A few minutes later I often heard him play a part of a Bach fugue on the specially constructed piano in his room which has pedals for organ practice. At other times, when I walked past his room from the dining room he was already bent over his table and by the light of his kerosene lamp submerged in the endless writing and reading which goes on until after midnight.

A few times I was kept busy and came late to dinner. I learned that part of the ritual is that you can come late as often as you like, provided you don't offer excuses.

"It is a rational procedure," Schweitzer explained to me. "Otherwise," he said, "I have to go constantly through this boring routine of: 'I'm sorry'—'it does not matter'—'don't mention it'—'Yes, but I could not help it'—'I hate to be late'—and so on ad infinitum."

Although he has the most exquisite manners one could expect of a gentleman of the Old World, he despises bowing and scraping before doors, shoving chairs under behinds, rising collectively when someone disappears to the "bathroom," and other such mechanical imitations of genuine politeness. Most of all he is irked when at a gathering he is offered the most comfortable chair. "I hate good manners," he says. What he really hates are the apelike automatic tricks we indulge in.

For some people the Hospital routine which precludes privacy becomes intolerable after a short while, and I think that all white inhabitants of the Hospital at times suffer from some degree of claustrophobia which may be expressed by irritability or suppressed rebellion.

Even in one's room there is no complete rest; the barrack-like building has been divided into rooms by very thin partitions. Actually they are cubicles rather than rooms, for the ceiling consists partly of mosquito screening and the space between it and the actual roof forms an ideal soundbox.

Nurses Devika and Almut, from the goodness of their hearts, keep sick babies in their rooms at night. Sick babies cry and I often had the feeling that they were crying somewhere under my bed. I heard whispered conversations five rooms away. I awoke whenever someone dropped his shoes on the floor anywhere in the building and heard the splashing of wash water from everywhere. When I turned around in my screeching bed I felt guilty of having awakened other light sleepers. The more private functions for which enamel apparatus is provided become a problem in delicacy. A little more privacy would make the Hospital more livable and efficient. Married couples, of course, cannot stand it for any length of time. People valuable to Lambaréné have no doubt been frightened away. Dr. Schweitzer, who has powers of concentration far beyond the ordinary, probably does not re-

The "Pharmacie"

alize this. He can sit at his little table in the "Pharmacie" with a hundred patients milling around and a deafening din going on everywhere, concentrating quietly on a letter which he is answering in his precise longhand or adding long columns of figures.

I have used the words ritual and ritualistic quite often. It should not be understood as criticism, for it is not. The Hospital has grown throughout its forty-five years and necessarily reflects the personality who created it from nothing and who for nearly half a century has been the only person continuously in charge with few and then only short interruptions. Even his oldest collaborators are comparative newcomers. No wonder innumerable customs originally started by common sense hardened into dogma. This is especially so because even now Dr. Schweitzer feels he carries the complete personal responsibility for the welfare of everyone of his guests and staff. This is no doubt the reason why, for example, he disapproves of long trips by speedboat or pirogue—there are dangers involved. It also explains the strict order to wear sun helmets from sunrise to sundown. The sun helmet has become a rather obsolete and unpopular part of tropical equipment. It fairly symbolizes colonialism. But it will protect one against sunstroke and there have been few fatal cases of sunstroke in the history of Lambaréné.

He does not like his staff to accept dinner invitations. I did not understand this until I saw the results of one such invitation. At the Hospital food is prepared under the strictest supervision. Vegetables and salads are soaked for hours in solutions of antiseptic. Schweitzer and his closest collaborators have not contracted tropical diseases although they have stayed in the tropics much longer than many others, and in the center of a puddle of infection more concentrated than perhaps anywhere on earth. During my stay one of the nurses developed an amoebic dysentery after a meal at a neighboring Mission. This potentially serious, and at best obstinate and debilitating, disease changed her in one day from a much needed asset into a difficult liability. So, many of the rituals seem to be firmly based on practical considerations. Nevertheless, I liked my periodical dive into potential infection and danger.

One of my patients was the manager of the Air France Hotel in Lambaréné. This hotel, strangely out of place in the little village where it stands, was probably built in the hope that it would attract American tourists coming to see the Phenomenon of Lambaréné. Monsieur Durivault, the young manager, is a creative artist and whether there are many guests or none, he puts into practice all he has learned at some sort of university for hotel people in Paris, especially his culinary art. He improvises with as much virtuosity on the tournedos à la Rossini as Schweitzer does on "Abide with Me." In gratitude for treatment in my clinic he came to fetch me on Sunday mornings and took me to his dining room. His improvisations were fantastic. He pulled out all stops of his culinary organ and served a dinner of six courses, three different wines, pâte de foie gras flown in from Strasbourg, truffels from Périgord, cheeses from Dauphiné, Brie, Chavignol, Roblochon, and Pont l'Évêque. The coda consisted usually of special concoctions of cream, cake, and liqueurs accompanied by a bottle of Heidsieck Extra Dry. Who but a Frenchman could tame the wilderness in this particular way?

In the evening, Durivault accompanied me on my way back upstream to the Hospital. From one of the small villages on the river banks the sound of the tom-toms came in waves across the water. As we approached, dancing figures were visible through the leaves of the banana trees. The dance was one of many survivals of old animistic rituals which persist under a Christian veneer.

"They do it every Sunday afternoon," my host explained. "Do you notice that only the men are dancing? Women are not even allowed to watch. My wife once innocently stopped to look, and she just escaped being beaten up."

The sun was setting and by the time we reached the Hospital it was nearly dark. The air was so full of mosquitoes that it seemed wise to take an extra antimalaria tablet. In the falling dusk African patients were cooking their meals on little wood fires behind the wards, each family for itself.

Groups of dark figures were singing psalms or chanting Ave Marias. A square, heavy-featured lay preacher was leading in prayer. Going up the steps to my room the urbane episode at Lambaréné's "Maxim's" already seemed unreal. The reality of the Hospital, of "Behold, all flesh is as the grass" swallowed me up like a tidal wave.

A Walk Through the Hospital

Before I came to Lambaréné I had seen many photographs and read many descriptions of the Hospital, but
I had never had a clear picture. Imagine accompanying
me on a morning's walk as I went drawing.

At the beach a stiff old man, coming from perhaps
two hundred miles away, was being lifted from a pirogue.
He looked desperately ill. He was placed on the sandy
beach of the river and some people were already shouting, "*Brancardiers, brancardiers!*" (stretcher-bearers). I
followed the old man, now lifted on a rough wooden
stretcher, along a path between the palm trees, leading
up the hill from the beach. Wide-eyed children were

On a rough wooden stretcher

playing about, a few convalescent patients strolled around leaning like patriarchs on tall staffs. Some wore only cotton trousers, others the traditional garb of large-patterned cotton, draped and tied around the neck and falling freely like a toga. A group of women was bargaining with fishermen for pieces of fish or crocodile. As I neared the Hospital, still following the stretcher, the crowd became denser. Women were sitting on steps suckling babies, a man strutted around in an old uniform and a peaked cap. A middle-aged man in a loincloth wore a sahib's sun helmet with great dignity. A strange woman of about fifty stared at me. She was completely nude except for a tiny apron, a big felt hat, and a machete.

"Who is she?" I asked an orderly. He told me that nobody speaks her language and that she is considered a little mad.

"She has been here for years," he said, "and she is quite harmless. We call her 'Maman-san-Nom.'"

In the first building on the right, the machine shed, a large generator and a smaller one were noisily making electricity for the operating rooms. The rest of the Hospital has kerosene lighting. The larger generator supplies the X-ray machine and is used sparingly. A hollow-cheeked Dutch mechanic, who stayed on in Lambaréné after a long illness, is in charge. He explained that Dr. Schweitzer gets very irritated if the large generator is used too long. He cannot stand the noise of the motor disturbing the tropical peace.

In front of the machine shed washerwomen were sitting in a big circle beating the hospital linen, their skirts tucked in (African women have a way of tucking in their skirts with great decorum leaving their legs completely bare), the tubs held firmly between muscular, well-formed thighs. On the left are a few long, low buildings —rough lumber shacks topped by red corrugated tin roofs. They are divided into cubicles. Each one is the habitat of an orderly or other helper, usually with his family. Also on the left is the warehouse from which food rations are distributed at regular times. The line of waiting people in front of it divided listlessly to let the stretcher pass. Next to the warehouse, between the palms, is a somewhat larger building which, although built many years ago, is still called the "New Ward," and which is always full of patients.

The man on the stretcher was now facing the rear of the "Pharmacie." "Pharmacie" is the traditional name of the whole complex of operating room, sterilizing room, dressing station, dental clinic, delivery room, and nursery. Actually it is the large hall which was the Hospital's original core. Drugs were dispensed here from the beginning, when it was also reception center, examining room, and dressing station. It still is. Against the window stands Dr. Schweitzer's old writing table.

In order to get inside, the man on the stretcher had first to be carried through a tunnel beneath the Pharmacie where three or four men were breaking up rocks with heavy hammers. (They are right underneath Schweitzer's table, so he can hear when they stop working and encourage them with his customary energy.) Then the patient was carried up a few concrete steps to what is called Main Street. From here he was taken into the Pharmacie and placed on one of the examining tables to wait until someone would take care of him.

Main street

Main Street forms a kind of valley. One side of the street consists of the Pharmacie. The other side is occupied by a two-storied barn, the top floor of which is a ward; the ground floor, a semi-basement, is used for the treatment of urological cases. Immediately behind the ward building the hillside rises sharply, leaving just enough space for the families of the patients to camp, cook, do their washing, and conduct their social life in immediate contact with their sick.

At both ends of Main Street rough steps lead out of the valley—at the far end to many clusters of cabins for African patients scattered in the greenery, at the opposite end along a branching path to three long barracks parallel on progressively higher terraces. The lowest contains eight rooms for white patients, the two higher ones house doctors, nurses, and guests. In the highest of the three, however, there is the equivalent of Lambaréné's "Waldorf Towers": a double room for visiting V. I. P.'s and their wives.

Along the path beside the three long buildings a huge church bell hangs from a steel structure. It is a present given to Schweitzer by the City of Dortmund on his eightieth birthday. There are also a few smaller bells and gongs used to call the staff to meals, the patients to Sunday worship, and everyone who can walk to the beach for arrivals and departures of importance.

At this point the Hospital proper ends and something like an old-fashioned European farm begins. The Schweitzer house is on the right of the farmyard, the kitchen for the staff on the left, and a low laundry shed nearly closes it off at the far end. But in the middle

Dr. Schweitzer's room

of the shed a rough archway leads to the path which continues to the river and the truck gardens. Along it stands what is known as "Hinter Indien," that world famous outhouse, final disillusion of dozens of fervent idealists who came to Lambaréné to find their vocation, a haloed saint, and modern plumbing.

The farmyard hums from sunset to sundown with tailors sewing, cobblers hammering, girls ironing, and oil lamps being cleaned and filled.

In the morning it is like a market: women bring fruits and manioc, work gangs are mustered and given tasks, steam shoots up from the laundry shed. Goats, chickens, and ducks loot the baskets, buckets, and sacks standing among the mangy palm trunks.

Through the window of the large wooden cabin which I call the Schweitzer house the Boss again is working quietly, sitting on his stool. There are no chairs. The rest of the house consists of the rooms of Mathilde Kottmann, Ali Silver, and a few girls of the housekeeping staff.

Just off the farmyard stands the only stone building: the communal dining room for the European staff. From its windows the eye roams beyond the enclosure for antelopes to two white crosses just under Schweitzer's window which mark the graves of Mrs. Schweitzer and Emma Hausknecht, the Hospital's first head nurse. Further on, across the Ogowe, endless stretches of forest mark the horizon.

Back of the dining room is the shower. It consists of a big bucket which you fill by pitcher with rain water, if there happens to be rain water in the cistern. The bucket is suspended from a rope and has a pierced bottom —no moving parts to go wrong. When the shower stops all you have to do is dry.

From the dining room a path leads to the Leper Village. At first it is a wide garden path lined by stables for the goats. Then, narrowing to a foot's width, it winds uphill and down, through meadows filled with grapefruit, orange, and breadfruit trees. Leading into the jungle, the path continues through ferns, palms, and strange big-leaved plants where something, wind or reptile, is always moving in the stillness. In the foliage along the path stand old gravestones of people who died at the Hospital. They have Christian, Moslem, and pagan markers. Deeper in the jungle, raw red earth is visible. Here newly dug graves can be seen. Many are healed, many die.

Into the jungle

How often did I walk that path! It was utterly quiet. Here and there little groups of goats chewed large leaves from the bushes; parrots, chattering busily, swooped down from the palms like flights of pigeons. Toucan-like birds made small excursions from the breadfruit trees in which they lived. Down the path old women carrying loads of sticks greeted me with a friendly "*Bolo*" (good morning) and with that beautiful open African smile which is in such contrast with the closed faces of Indians I had met on similar walks in Mexico. And often I met Maman-sans-Nom, her nude, heavy body suddenly emerging from the undergrowth, machete at the ready. I always said, "*Bolo*," and bowed politely. And she answered with an angry monologue. I tried to remember that she was "quite harmless" but quickened my step to where the path widened into an unpaved street lined with raffia huts. Here the Leper Village began. . . .

The Leper Village

Leprosy in our consciousness is still associated with the ill-defined dread disease of the Bible and with the bell-ringing outcasts of the Middle Ages, when all kinds of skin diseases were lumped together under this name. Leprosy, or as it is now often called, Hansen's disease, is about the least catching of all contagious diseases. No one knows exactly how contagion with Hansen's micro-bacillus takes place. Sometimes white workers have become infected, but these cases are rare and a special predisposition seems to be required. Since 1941, and thanks to an American scientist, Dr. Guy Faget, effective drugs, the sulfones, have come into use which make it probable that this horrible social scourge can be converted into a purely medical problem and eradicated within our lifetime. True, there are individuals who do not respond to the sulfones, but newer drugs give hope that for them, too, cure can be obtained. In most cases, provided an early diagnosis is made, mutilations can be prevented.

In Africa, the sulfones have been in use only since the early 1950's, and hence one still finds innumerable persons who show the leonine features, the missing fingers and toes, and the unspeakable wounds of the classical leper. With the new drugs, new attitudes were introduced and leper villages became less and less something like garbage cans for leprous mankind.

Treatment became part of the system of mass and preventive medicine now in operation all over Africa. Early diagnosis and the simplicity of administration of sulfones make it possible to treat most patients at local dispensaries. Statistics of the World Health Organization show that there is more than ninety per cent regular attendance. There is no better propaganda for any treatment than cure!

Who, then, now inhabit these leper villages? First, patients who do not react normally to drugs; then, those who are still contagious and would be a threat to their communities; lastly, those whose mutilations had already progressed so far before the advent of the sulfones that they are helpless. When one thinks of isolation of lepers one should eliminate any idea of enclosures or barbed-wire entanglements. Very often I met inhabitants of the Village on the river, who would wave to me as we went in separate pirogues to Lambaréné-Downtown. The newer ideal of "isolation" is not the illusory hundred per cent segregation from which patients would escape anyway, but effective control of contagious patients.

The Schweitzer Leper Village is new. The Grand Docteur built it with the money he received along with the Nobel Prize for Peace. It consists of a main road lined by neat raffia huts on concrete foundations, in which the inhabitants are housed comfortably. The road slopes down gently to the Casa Lagerfelt, its social and medical center, a gift of one of Schweitzer's closest friends, the Swedish Baroness Lagerfelt. It contains a treatment room and a little laboratory where constant checks are made on the contagiousness of patients.

The whole Village is surrounded by jungle but the road continues to the beach of the Ogowe where remains of the original Leper Village are still standing. Along the beach lie the usual clusters of pirogues which one finds in any village on the Ogowe. The Village is a community with community service. It is kept immaculate by the collective work of the inmates and their children. Its orderlies are inmates, its pastor is a very sick patient who, besides leprosy, has a heart disease. The Village is an almost self-contained unit with a stable population. Medically it is supervised by one of the doctors of the Hospital. Unfortunately there is no leprologist in charge, but the impossible is being done by that very hardworking, reed-thin, and blonde bundle of energy and enthusiasm, the Swiss nurse Trudi. She treats, dominates, teaches, and mothers this whole community of two hundred people and I believe that it is she who has welded it into the unit it has become. It is she who each morning disinfects and treats the deep, repulsive wounds on the bodies of her people without a thought for her own safety. She seems to feel responsible for the entire life of each person in her whole little empire. She slaps, consoles, and spoils the children as though she were the Great Mother herself. When it was arranged that I would examine and treat the whole Village, it was Trudi who organized to perfection the whole set-up in the little Village Square —between the Casa Lagerfelt and the huts and the jungle —where she also has her dressing station under the big trees.

Weeks before I had started to treat the inhabitants of the Village I had begun to draw them. People everywhere in the world resent being photographed by camera-toting tourists. They feel that the man with the camera sees them as mere bit players in his amateur production and they resent it. But they enjoy being drawn. Whether in the slums of Marseille or in an African leper village, the fellow who sits quietly in a corner drawing with a pen on a piece of paper becomes a sort of magician and friend. The onlookers start to recognize their houses, their neighbors, and their children, and become more and more interested. They soon feel that they are not being caricatured, but that the act of drawing is one of respect, an intensive seeking of contact with their world.

After watching me draw for a few mornings, some of the older women, gaping at my first sketches, asked me whether I could not teach them "the trick." The children brought me their tame stork, Mombambra, to draw. I was already known as the "Tooth-Doctor-Who-Draws," and a bond of friendship was established.

Once I have drawn people and am forced to concentrate on them individually, they no longer form a mass. The contact established is not a collective one, but a firm personal rapport with Albert, Augustine, Luc, Lazare, Henriette.

Drawing is a probing of reality by eye and hand combined. It is a way of coming closer to Reality. Nature everywhere waits to be drawn, for it is an act of love which even animals sense. Something in the artist and in the monkey makes wordless contact. Is that why all children still in unbroken relationship to reality can draw, and draw well? Is it because they lose this close touch when they grow up and become enclosed in their ego-shell, that they "can't draw a straight line?" Once I have drawn something, it seems to become part of my inner life forever. I have taken possession of a world, without holding on to it. Perhaps it was the drawing that made me forget that by the color of my skin and my training I was different from my friends in the Leper Village. Even groups of laughing tourists, snapping pictures, seemed to consider me part of the backdrop, as though I had been made invisible by my absorption.

But, first, more about the children. Were they all lepers? No. Of the twenty children, perhaps five were infected. Only one, little Jean, bore the obvious marks on his ears; and fifteen-year-old Albert, a highly sensitive and wonderful boy who later became one of my best drawing pupils, had one leprous foot amputated, an ill-conceived "treatment" by a misinformed doctor.

The rest of the children were living here because their parents were confined to the Village. It may seem a little surprising that healthy children are left with leprous parents, but it has been found everywhere that child mortality increases enormously when children are separated from their parents; and the chances of infection are comparatively low.

Two children did not really belong in the Village at all. For little Henriette, a twelve-year-old lovable child with a congenital heart disease, the more stable environment of the Village was thought preferable to the ever-shifting population of the Hospital. Seven-year-old Augustine really looked quite healthy, but she, too, had been born with a bad heart and had not much chance of survival.

The children of the Village seemed to be especially gifted for singing. They had an extensive repertory of French songs which they performed like a trained choir at the strangest moments. The weakest stimulus was enough to start a performance. When they heard my first name was Frederick, they spontaneously started, "*Je m'appelle Frédéric*," a lusty song they had known a long time. But I was the first "Frédéric" they knew and so it became my private "Marseillaise" or "Star-Spangled Banner." They started singing it as soon as I made my appearance. One great advantage of this was that I no longer was *le docteur* but simply Frédéric. And it was Frédéric who gave his drawing lessons every Sunday after worship. For suddenly everyone wanted to draw.

Drawing lessons actually don't exist at all. People draw if they can, the way they breathe, sing, or make love. A teacher has only to give them paper, pencils, and crayons and remind them of their ability to draw. At first they'll start to scribble unhappily until you mention a subject from their own environment. "Draw the Hospital! Draw me! Draw Trudi! Draw people in a pirogue! Draw the stork!" Before I realized it they were off. They drew people chasing crocodiles, snakes winding around palm trees, pelicans gobbling fish. As always I asked myself who had "talent" and who had not. People draw what they are! Almost everybody joined in, from the youngest to the middle-aged.

Victor, a young intellectual looking man who had hardly any fingers left and whose feet were totally mutilated and bandaged, drew holding a pencil between the bandaged stumps of his hands. Victor had a most vivid imagination. Almost miraculously, he carved a beautiful native harp for me later.

Old Marc was the most gifted designer, with something of Mondriaan's geometrical sense. He also sculpted beautiful animals and heads in his spare time.

Luc did not draw. He had been a leper from boyhood. At first sight his face appeared to be a face from a nightmare. The nose had widened into a monstrous cluster of black fruits, the brow thickened by leprous growths, the eyes yellow and swollen, feet and hands repulsive. Luc is Trudi's best orderly. He works all day, dressing the wounds of his fellow lepers, giving injections, and nursing the children. Once you are used to the cruel joke played by nature on Luc, you notice to your great surprise a kind of beauty in him. Nature made a caricature of his face, but his humanity shines through it in a touching smile, in tenderness for the children, in composure when he is racked with pain. For Luc suffers from the terrible neuralgias which so often are part of leprosy. After I had treated him he appeared the next day holding an egg in his hand as a present. On my assistant's birthday, when Luc himself was too ill to walk from the Village to the Hospital, he sent one of the children with a bunch of field flowers.

Sometimes he is acutely ill. In leprosy occur those relapses in which the illness suddenly becomes reactivated. Then Luc has high fever and is deeply depressed, depressed most of all because he cannot work. It is his work which gives him his self-respect. As soon as he is a little better he hobbles around and is active again, helping others. "It is the heart that commands," he says, "not the body."

Djibadi, a wizened pock-marked little man, an excellent orderly although he was hardly able to walk on his leprous feet, had the gay color sense of a French impressionist, something Renoir-ish. The most stupid of all, Mjukanji, who looked at you with great protruding dog's eyes, to my great surprise drew only camels. I later found out that he had a cutout wooden toy camel, which he held against the paper and outlined with his pencil, after which he colored his "drawing." He was not always sure which side of the camel was up because he had never seen a camel, but this made his design the more modern and interesting. When I praised him for his art work the big eyes filled with tears of gratitude. One day the miracle happened and Mjukanji started to draw, without benefit of toy camel, anything that came into his head; the well of creativity had opened up and was flowing.

We decided to make a large collective mural, nearly

the whole Village participating. I got a huge piece of drawing paper, about six by eight feet. Marc made the divisions. Victor was asked to do the lower part because he could not stand and had to be carried on his little stool to where the paper was stretched against the wall of a hut. One-footed Albert wanted to draw Le Grand Docteur with one of his pelicans. According to talent and age, spaces were allotted to be filled in by everyone who wanted to. There was great general enthusiasm and our first completed mural amazed Le Grand Docteur himself, who had never suspected such talent among his lepers.

The second mural was never finished. A few of my collaborators became very ill. For reasons which are not well understood, sufferers of leprosy at times get what is known as "lepromatous reactions" in which the disease suddenly flares up and the patient suffers from high fever, general prostration, and often great pain. It is possible that a vaccination which took place around this time had brought about this reaction among some of my friends. When I left they were still ill.

The collective work with the Leper Village and the close rapport which had developed made it difficult for me to leave Lambaréné. On my last evening, in the dark outside the dining room, a choir suddenly struck up "*Je m'appelle Frédéric.*" I left the table to shake hands with the singers. I was glad it was dark and they could not see the tears in my eyes.

The Tooth-Doctor-Who-Draws

*A*s it turned out, I drew a lot. Both pictures and, God knows, teeth. In my few months at Lambaréné I saw some five to six hundred patients, did hundreds of fillings, extractions, operations, treatments. I also taught some dental procedures to the staff—emergency dentistry. For real, professional dentistry is a very complex branch of, respectively, medicine, artistry, engineering, and practical psychology. The average physician has no idea of dental procedures and if I were forced to choose between having a baby delivered by a dentist or a wisdom tooth extracted by an obstetrician I would just toss a coin.

It is high time, however, that courses in emergency

dentistry be given to doctors, nurses, and missionaries, who have to serve in areas where they are called upon to relieve dental suffering. This *must* be done, I feel, for I learned in Africa that dentistry is not the marginal profession it might appear to be in America, a dilly-dallying with aesthetics and a radiant smile. Dental suffering is in no way secondary to any other suffering. Dental help is as essential as any other medical help. The need for dental help is perhaps best illustrated by the story of an American missionary's wife who had heard about my clinic. News of this kind spreads fast over hundreds of miles even though no one has a telephone. The missionary and his wife immediately took their truck and traveled for two whole days over unspeakable forest roads to Lambaréné. My work consisted of a simple extraction! Afterward the woman told me what she had gone through. For over a year she had been suffering periodically from horrible toothaches. A few months ago she had become so desperate that she hired bearers and walked seventy miles to see a doctor who, she was told, did some dentistry. The truck at the time was out of commission because of a spare part which had to come from America. She reached the doctor's hospital after walking for days and was told that the doctor had just left for Europe. She returned the whole way again on foot with her retinue and her toothache, camping in government shelters. Intermittently she continued to suffer from almost unbearable toothaches until the day she came to Lambaréné.

Another missionary arrived after a trip of many hours by speedboat down the Ogowe River with an equally simple case. He lived on a remote post; his agonies had gone on for two years ever since he had returned from European leave. His European physician had told him he was suffering from neuralgia and had given him medication. Although the poor man had been poisoning himself for two years with barbiturates, his pain continued. The mysterious "neuralgia" disappeared as by magic when I extracted a tooth with an obvious chronic abscess.

A doctor at the Hospital had considerable pain and a dangerous inflammatory swelling which had to be controlled constantly with antibiotics. Surgical removal of an impacted and infected wisdom tooth made it possible for him to go back to his indispensable work.

These are just a few examples of what happened every day.

In order to start my clinic I first had to find the money, make precise lists of necessary supplies, order

Dr. Schweitzer checks arrival of supplies

them, pack them, go through all formalities, and send them off a month before I left myself. By air, of course, to make sure; it would be worth the extra expense. I arrived at Lambaréné and found nothing, not even a bill of lading. I explained, inquired, and cajoled. Everybody shrugged his shoulders in French colonial resignation, expressed by the French shrug with added colonial emphasis.

"Oh," they said, "maybe a month, maybe two months. Your stuff is probably lying in Douala in the Cameroons or at Port-Gentil or Libreville, in a customs shed. You know, we are understaffed here, and it is hot and one has to take these things philosophically. It will come, don't worry. Maybe it will even come before you leave!"

But then, I came from New York. I wanted action. There was, however, not even that frantic substitute for action, the telephone. But I could cable to New York and to all the African places I could think of. This waste of money amused everybody very much and made them shrug more. Meanwhile, in the labyrinthian stockrooms of Schweitzer's Hospital I had been finding things. There is not much you can look for that you don't eventually find in those subterranean treasure houses: all the good surgeons who have sent their old instruments to help poor Schweitzer, retired dentists who sent grosses of the most fantastic extraction forceps with so little relationship to human teeth that they were probably designed for hippos or leopards. Nothing is thrown away. I found enough to set up a semblance of a clinic and I was able to start work on the second day. Patients streamed in—black, white, and in-between—and for good luck I had among my first emergencies the wife of one of the airline representatives in the region, and a high government official.

Now it was my turn to shrug *à la française* and say: "Sorry, but my instruments have been lying somewhere at the customs in Port-Gentil, Libreville, or Douala for a month or so. I can't treat your particular trouble without them."

These two patrician toothaches came no doubt straight from Heaven—but then, I believe that Dr. Schweitzer's Hospital has often been helped by special divine intervention. Within two days my equipment arrived by government launch from Lambaréné.

My clinic was situated in the main building, the Pharmacie. I had a little cubbyhole flanked on the left by the dressing station where emergency operations were also performed and from which I was separated by a cardboard partition. To the right of my chair was a similar partition, open at the top, separating me from the Delivery Room! Part of my own domain, used as a waiting room, contained examining tables, and a curtain could be drawn across so that dentistry and gynecology were at any rate symbolically separated. In the far corner stood the cradle of a baby which had probably a tubercular meningitis. It had been in coma for over a month and was being fed intravenously.

On the side of the dressing station there was a second gap in the partition, also precariously closed off by a white sheet. Behind it was the consulting cubicle of *Doctoresse*, who at her little desk was taking histories in curious mixtures of French, Dutch, and Gabonese dialects.

My own domain

I don't have to describe the clinic itself, just look at the picture. Sitting in the dental chair my patient looked out of the window and had a more exciting view than if he had come to my New York office: among the palm trees people were milling, children playing, dogs barking, and goats busy in their eternal quest for food. On the shining river speedboats screamed and pirogues drifted toward the landing bringing in new patients. To the right one could see the shed where food rations were being distributed and where men, women, and children were queuing up. Of course the word window has to be understood in the African sense; instead of glass it was made of mosquito screening.

To form an idea of the din going on, imagine that a painful injection is being given in a dressing station on your left and that *Doctoresse* is trying to make her questions understood by that involuntary raising of the voice she uses in the vain hope that shouting will make her meaning clearer. On the right, either a delivery is in progress or a baby's first cry is accompanied by the enthusiastic singsonging and stamping of female relatives, dancing around the delivery table. At that moment the lovely Swiss midwife, gripped by the spirit, storms into my office to show me the newest and most thrilling sample of African population! In front, the bells are ringing (bells are constantly ringing) to call attention to the distribution of rations, medicaments, or what have you; children are romping and palavers are passionately being pursued. In my "waiting room" patients chat and try to draw me into their fascinating conversations through the curtain. As in the continuo in the *St. Matthew Passion*, there is the rhythmic hammering of three or four men who underneath my office are breaking up large rocks into small gravel used for the repair of local paths. A sort of oboe aria is constantly heard above it all, the nasal voice of the Hungarian doctor, two rooms away, who likes to reproach his patients for infractions of hospital etiquette, threatening them with expulsion, withholding of rations, or worse. After a few days this infernal noise no longer bothered me. It only made me sit up straight in bed in the middle of the night, re-enacted in a nightmare.

My patients fell into three categories. I felt it my first duty to come to the dental rescue of the staff, and for them alone I could have worked a year. What makes people's teeth go so unbelievably bad during a few years in Africa? Probably the high carbohydrate diet and a certain laxity in hygiene promote decay. Besides, a lack of vitamins leads to gum diseases and pyorrhea. Add to this a complete absence of dental care and very often only a sketchy overhaul before leaving Europe or America. The less I say about the few dentists in the area, each about an hour's flight away, the better.

First members of the staff of the Hospital, both European and native, were scheduled and, of course, its Chief. "Just come and get me when you have time. That is, if the females will let me off for a few minutes," he added with a wink in the direction of the devoted elderly lady who was checking bills with him. As one would expect, he was the most correct and considerate patient of all, and insisted on paying me with an enormous elephant's wisdom tooth.

The next category were "whites" from the neighborhood. This neighborhood stretched to about an hour by plane, eight hours by speedboat, or a couple of days by truck. My most distinguished patient was a judge who honored my skill by flying in twice from Port-Gentil. Most of these people presented dental problems hardly ever met with in America, the accumulated result of years of neglect. All I could hope to do was to restore them to a relative degree of dental health, so that, at any rate, they could await their next European leave free from dental catastrophe.

I did not charge for my treatments, but asked the Hospital to make a more or less symbolic charge for overhead. In practically every case the fee was reduced to almost nothing for fear of overcharging. An extensive treatment, during which the patient sometimes lived at the Hospital for five days or so, might cost all of thirty-five dollars. It is typical of the Hospital to charge in pennies rather than dollars, and probably some schedule of fees of the early nineteen hundreds is still in operation, blandly ignoring all inflations, deflations, crashes, and recessions we—and the French franc—have gone through.

Usually my white patients were extraordinarily grateful and appreciative, expressing their feelings in offerings of gorilla skulls, dinners, elephants' teeth, and trips on the Ogowe. But there were some snooty, blonde wives of lumber executives, accustomed to exaggerated over-evaluation by every white male. I found that one way to get rid of such a conceited female was to give her tooth-brushing instructions in a row with six black college students from the Mission next door. The Missions were my third and perhaps most important field of action: the native population.

Hospital patients had first priority. They soon knew that they could come whenever they had pain. A few of them decided to try me out. They complained about improbable pains all over and explained the strange radiations of their discomfort as all Africans always do: by making strange jumping motions with the tips of their fingers along the presumed path of pain and crowing "*cu-cu-cu-cu-cu-cu-cu.*" Taking a leaf out of their own book of magic, I would take an inky solution of methylene blue, fold my hands solemnly, look at the place where the "*cu-cu-cu-cu-cu-cu-cu*" was taking place, and paint the spot dark blue. The patients were deeply impressed with the blue saliva they spat and often I could proudly point to miraculous and instantaneous cures by this potent magic.

Where the source of pain seemed more rationally explicable, the only cure all too often was extraction, which was done in the Fifth Avenue manner with careful asepsis and anesthesia. My patients were amazed. Whole groups would stand in front of my clinic showing with fervent gestures how this great magician had managed to take a tooth the size of a carp out of their heads without any pain whatsoever.

Apart from the Hospital patients, I treated the whole Leper Village. I did not dare to mix them too obviously with other patients and one day examined the whole population of over two hundred in the Village itself. All inhabitants, including the smallest children, had been assembled on the "Square" where benches had been placed for them. With the help of Trudi and her leper assistants, instruments were sterilized and statistics recorded so that in one hectic afternoon all mouths were charted under the fierce eye of Mombambra, the stork. When I left, my private "Marseillaise" was sung by the children and the next day I returned to give treatments, which, alas, were again mostly extractions.

The easiest ones were done right in the "Square" where I read in my patients' eyes that their friend, the artist, had transformed himself into a figure of terror. All of a sudden I saw myself through their eyes, strutting

Children in the Leper Village

around in my huge surgical gown, rubber gloves, sun helmet, and glasses. I was dismayed but I had to continue, and as I went on working as painlessly and carefully as I could I gratefully noticed that soon I began to, look human again to my friends.

The mass treatment perhaps shocked me more than it did my patients, who are used to receiving medication en masse and to having their leprosy wounds dressed in public ón the "Square." But it made me so uncomfortable that I transferred the leper practice to my clinic, whether the Administrator, Juge d'Instruction, or Commissaire de District, liked it or not.

As a sort of public relations project for Dr. Schweitzer and his Hospital, I branched out to the Catholic and Protestant Missions of the District. On separate days I took a pirogue, loaded it with mouth mirrors, probes, flashlight, and paper for statistics and went to look at, respectively, Catholic and Protestant teeth.

The Catholic teeth were under the supervision of a dignified and gracious Mother Superior who had already entrusted her own to me as well as those of some of her nuns. One of the Sisters came from Paraguay and was in the possession of a single unstable tooth which she implored me to save. I tried all within my human power for the poor tooth, but told her that I couldn't promise anything. "*Il faut prier,*" I advised her in order to remain in style!

The African girls at the Convent ranged from seven to about nineteen. It was amazing how little tooth decay I found in these girls from the Lambaréné neighborhood, and it was a pleasure to make those few shiny silver fillings for them which no doubt doubled their price in the marriage market.

The Protestant Mission, however, was an entirely different affair. No charming nuns from Paraguay, no ceremonious Mothers Superior, no nice bottles of wine and leathery cookies in the refectory. To get to the Mission I paddled a couple of miles upstream on the Ogowe until I saw some new stucco buildings on the hillside above the palm trees. A rather derelict little church, which looks a hundred years old but seems to have been built around 1935, stands on the river bank. Andende, as the station is called, was founded by Americans some eighty years ago. In 1913, Dr. and Mrs. Schweitzer set up their first hospital here. Schweitzer's old house of classical colonial style is still standing.

A few hard-working, underpaid young French missionaries live here with their wives and pale children. They try their utmost to teach some two hundred and fifty native college students. When he is graduated, the student usually has the self-esteem of a double Ph.D. and the scholastic standing of a fourth-grader.

My dental examinations yielded some interesting scientific results. I found that all students originating north of a line running from Ogowe Trindo to Ogowe Estuaire showed massive decay, usually of all molars and most front teeth. By contrast, the students coming from the south of this demarcation line showed hardly any decay at all. These findings dispose neatly of the fairy tales about the excellent teeth of Africans and pose at the same time some very interesting questions regarding the cause of decay. Superficial conclusions are worse than none, and the only factual differences I found were that the people from the south have fish as a staple food whereas those from the north subsist mostly on manioc, peanuts, sugar cane, and some meat. But it would be most worth while to make a comparative study of these regions in terms of nutrition, soil, water, and other factors which might shed light on the causal factors in tooth decay.

The boys and girls were very co-operative. I treated them as ladies and gentlemen and found they responded completely, behaving as ladylike and gentlemanly as any white youngsters of their age could have. They were eager to receive treatment, sensitive and polite. Some of them even decided to stay on after their vacation had started, just to be treated. There was only one boy of about seventeen who barked at me and I nearly shouted back. Then I noticed that what I took for rudeness was not arrogance but an exceptionally strong stutter which he tried desperately to control. Ogoula Henri, about the most sensitive and intelligent of them all, became a real friend, a grateful patient, and, in a way, my public relations officer.

In retrospect, the only explanation for my great productivity can be found in the spirit of Lambaréné, where everyone seems to work far beyond human capacity, and especially in the extraordinary human rapport I had from the very beginning with the lovable people of Gabon.

The Lambaréné Landscape

All over the world, when Lambaréné is mentioned, one thinks of the Schweitzer Hospital sitting snugly in a steaming jungle. But once you are at the Hospital, Lambaréné recedes somewhere to the far horizon or even a little farther, for Lambaréné-Downtown is around the big bend in the Ogowe. Only a little suburb of a few huts is visible from the Hospital beach.

To place the Hospital in its physical environment let's start with a visit to Lambaréné-Downtown. Some devoted workers at the Hospital are so absorbed in their tasks that in their ten years at the Hospital they have never set foot into Lambaréné-Downtown. Dr.

Schweitzer himself rarely goes to Lambaréné except on official business. But I loved to go there at least once a week to buy a bottle of cognac for the long, hot, winter evenings. Also to refresh memories of real steak at the Air France Hotel, which in its modern architecture sticks out like an Empire State Building above the low huts and houses. Or to have a drink with that genial, rotund, and bearded potentate, the Chef de District, on his wide verandah overlooking the immense Ogowe landscape.

The village of Lambaréné is some three miles downstream from the Hospital and although once in a while I could get a lift in a speedboat arriving there so quickly I could see nothing, my normal way was to hire a pirogue with two or more rowers and spend a half-hour or so making the trip. From the Hospital the pirogue crossed

Lambaréné—Downtown

the Ogowe and the crew shouted greetings across the water to all other piroguers within earshot. Then we followed the high bank of the river.

Tropical trees dip nests of branches into the water. Tall palms line the road which, following the river, starts at a promontory, leads to the Catholic Mission with its French provincial chapel, and finally to the first houses of Lambaréné itself. Above the bushes and the high grass of the riverbank, dark heads could be seen bobbing. Here and there appeared women who, with babies strapped to their backs, balanced enamel basins of vegetables and household articles on their heads. Their colorful wraps flashed through the greenery. As we approached Lambaréné-Downtown more heads bobbed, including male ones often with the skullcaps of Moslem traders. My rowers stopped at the town landing where the ferry to the airport was loaded and unloaded, and where a hundred pirogues, rowboats, and motorboats were always moored. I climbed the riverbank opposite the big general store of Hatton & Cookson, Ltd., one of the biggest in Lambaréné. Hatton & Cookson, who started one of the first stores here, must have been two adventurous British traders of the nineteenth century. The name should not be pronounced in English, but in colonial French: Attonn et Coxonn! Next to Attonn et Coxonn stands a little white building, a machine shop built in mock seventeenth-century Dutch style as somebody's private joke. Spread over the hills are a few hundred houses and huts, ranging from simple straw structures via bourgeois villas to the splendors of the Hotel and the Government House at the top. In the hills I visited the government hospital with one overworked doctor for the whole District. Apart from his medical work he has to fill in reams of statistics and probably operates with his right hand, while his left wields a fountain pen. On the way to the hospital I passed the gendarmerie with fezzed, black personnel loitering at the gate and one white gendarme at his desk inside.

Along the river are a number of garages and general stores, which like Attonn et Coxonn lack shop windows and are simply large sheds filled with diverse merchandise. Behind the L-shaped counter African salesmen unhurriedly chatted with their customers. From a little office the wakeful eye of a fat Frenchman or a corpulent Madame roamed constantly over the counter and the shelves. I bought my bottle and cookies in the stores managed by those who came by pirogue to my clinic for treatment. I was received with deference and often got as much as a hundred per cent reduction on the price of my cognac.

Later I usually sent the pirogue back to wait for me at the promontory while I walked through the village and then for a few miles along the palm-lined road, which looked like an endless baroque church interior with sculptured pillars and ornamented roof. The first mile through Downtown was always crowded with people. Since everybody knew that I was the Tooth-Doctor-Who-Draws, I got solemn and respectful greetings. On the right the shining river was always alive with pirogues, old steamboats, and huge rafts piled with mahogany and floating downstream to the Delta, the crews and their families camping on the tree trunks. On the left there is

a long row of straw huts and rough little wooden shan-
ties, each one a little shop exhibiting in front, on a few
shaky tables, a little manioc, a few onions, cheap jewelry,
rubber enema syringes, native medicines, naphthalene
balls, dresses and little clay pipes for the ladies, and cigarettes to be sold individually. The more prosperous
shops are owned by long-robed Sudanese whom I had
difficulty drawing because of their Moslem distaste for
portraiture.

Then the village ended and the palms and tangled
bushes in all varieties of green took over.

Near the Catholic Mission I chatted politely with a
few strolling nuns in white. A little Negro girl in a stiff
white organdy frock, surrounded by proud parents and
relatives in their Sunday best, was returning from First
Communion. The gendarme saluted as if I were the flag.
In the distance a red-bearded padre was reading his breviary. Gradually I felt as though I had become part of a
charming engraving illustrating life in the colonies around
1850. Invaded by a complete sense of timeless reality, I
sleepwalked on. Near the promontory on the many little
beaches families were sitting with their pirogues half
drawn on the hot sand, the men staring out over the
water, the women suckling babies and calling to their
other children who were romping in the sand. And there
was my boat waiting with Obiange, the oarsman, waving
his hat and shouting, "Here we are, Docteur!"

Smoothly the dugout drifted over the calm river to
the clamorous contemporary reality of the Hospital. Although one cannot get to Schweitzer's Hospital by car,
one can get very close to it. I often walked the half-mile

to the east to a little boatyard belonging to a lumber dealer who ships his rafts with his own modern tugboat to Port-Gentil. There I felt as though I had stepped into the twentieth century. Black mechanics were working efficiently, repairing boat motors. In a modern house with radio, electric lights, and running water the quite contemporarily nervous owner lives his colonial life. Of course he has trucks and the inevitable jeeplike car. Another jeep belonged to our neighbor on a side stream, also a patient, of course. He was a Teutonic looking Frenchman from Alsace, who also had an important lumber business. One morning he was waiting at the limit of the Hospital grounds, which is as far as you can get by car. Monsieur Boltz had come to take me about ten miles over a road, which for African conditions was not too bad, to his concession, a stretch of forest about forty miles in diameter peopled with gorillas, elephants, and especially valuable mahogany and okoumé trees. He showed with pride how these giant trees were felled and dragged by huge caterpillar tractors from deep gulleys in the virgin forests to a clearing where they were sorted and cut. Immense trucks would transport the lumber from deep in the forest, past his charming house, to the river where rafts were loaded. The roads through his property were narrow. Monsieur Boltz knew his truck schedule more or less by heart and often waited patiently for half an hour until one of his mammoths had passed full speed along the winding roads where visibility was close to zero.

At his home his charming and cultivated wife had prepared the kind of lunch you would expect in a good

Paris restaurant. The house consisted of a row of open hutlike structures with high gabled roofs; a dining-living hut simply and tastefully furnished. The kitchen was a separate hut, so was the bathroom, the office, and the washhouse. There was also, according to government regulation, a separate guesthouse, so that travelers stranded in the forest or passing by could find shelter for the night. On the other side of the road stood the technical installations—garages, workshops, generators, gasoline tanks. It looked like a small, well-organized village, where Monsieur Boltz was the mayor and his white mechanic and a few other employees his aldermen. Twentieth century again, although without running water and without a gas range. All cooking is done on wood fires, bread baked daily in clay ovens; yet it is still twentieth-century life in virgin forest, complete with kerosene refrigerator and radio, but without jitters.

The next Sunday I took a rowboat to Lake Zille, a few miles upstream, with five oarsmen, Chief Obiange in front of the boat, the others singing spontaneously in high soprano and deep bass under a nearly black sky. Following the Ogowe upstream, we soon saw a small gap in the vegetation on the right bank. It proved to be a small side stream, just wide enough for our flat-bottomed boat to get through. Tropical jungle formed walls you could touch with your hand and a low roof arched overhead. Unexpectedly we met piroques with native couples coming back from a fishing trip, the woman sitting in front. Polite greetings were exchanged and the pirogues were steered into the vegetation to let our bigger boat pass.

After a mile or so of this grotto-like channel the little stream widened and the boat drifted into a huge, dark lake strewn with many islands, some with a cluster of tiny huts, palm trees, or a single huge kapok tree. Other islands looked under the threatening sky like Boecklin's "Isle of the Dead" in the Metropolitan Museum. But these were far from isles of the dead. Everywhere fishermen in pirogues were throwing out nets. Shouts sounded across the water and Obiange called, *"Biba zoegem eleba."* ("We are just looking at the lake.") In other words: "No fishing competition!" From endless distances answers echoed over the water.

All at once a pirogue shot toward us. Its huge, savage looking nude owner, his somber primordial face lifted, was waving something in the air.

"C'est Jean-Baptiste Njange," explained Obiange, *"il te veut donner cadeau."*

The pirogue pulled up beside our boat, the huge man thrust a big living carp into my hands and spat out words, "Docteur save my wife, Njange thanks."

I dropped the poor jumping carp, made gestures of profound thanks, automatically offered cigarettes.

This hurt Njange. He waved his enormous arms in refusal, looked frighteningly insulted, and shouted, *"Non, moi cadeau pour Docteur,"* and shot away in his pirogue.

We killed the gaping fish and paddled back. Apparently Njange's wife had been operated at the Hospital and a white Docteur is a white Docteur.

Kingfishers and eagles dived from leaden clouds into the black water. Obiange pointed out a crocodile's snout sticking up a small distance away. The soprano singer continued his coloratura song, sounding like a mandolin, as we drifted homeward. I gave the rowers a few hundred francs as a *cadeau*, but the singer followed me and explained he'd like some more money in order to buy a wallet to put his francs in. I laughed and told him that this was a complex problem for him to solve.

"Either," I said, "you buy a wallet and then you have nothing to put into it, or, *eh bien*, you buy no wallet and keep the money in your pocket."

He looked inconsolable, but said what they always say, "*Oui, Docteur,*" and I gave him two cigarettes.

Dr. Schweitzer is opposed to his patients' smoking cigarettes in the Hospital. He insists correctly that if they have money to buy cigarettes, they should be able to buy their own food. Yet just because of this, the gift of a cigarette in appreciation of services became a powerful symbol of fellowship and solidarity.

People in the Landscape

The whites have given the dark microcosm of Lambaréné its stamp, its special Lambaréné form. But only its form. The universal themes of birth, adolescence, of desire and fulfillment, of inevitable sickness, old age, and, decay are developed in African tonality.

For the Hospital's leitmotiv is human suffering and transiency. A thousand variations on it are played every hour of the day and night. The variations on the theme are African, but the theme is universal. "How effective is this Hospital really?" I asked myself many times. In terms of the suffering of a continent it is obviously impotent. Yet each life saved, each pain stilled, each wound dressed, every bit of comfort given where no more help is possible, justifies it amply.

No hospital is better than its doctors. At the Schweitzer Hospital, as anywhere else, the quality of the doctors varies as to skill, insight, devotion, and rapport with patients. Here in the jungle the highest skill cannot mask a lack of human or medical judgment. Schweitzer may be gruff at times, but his compassion and his inexhaustible reservoirs of good will always shine through. And all patients feel it and revere him. On the other hand, they take him for granted. The Grand Docteur has become part of the Lambaréné landscape. Some of his assistants are of the highest human caliber and the patient placed in their hands is cared for as a beloved relative. Others, of course, have less skill, less feeling of responsibility, less self-criticism, and less human depth. Since the Schweitzer Hospital has to lack the technical means which are normal in any Western hospital, these individual qualities are of ultimate importance.

Quality in the doctors here seems to vary more than in the nurses. The latter form a homogeneous group of women who do their difficult work with complete and selfless devotion. The future—whoever may have to decide about the African future—will not be able to dispense with purely curative hospitals such as Dr. Schweitzer's, but must integrate them into the vast network of preventive medical services already in operation all over Africa. In the Belgian Congo I witnessed the impressive achievement of a comparatively small medical cadre which had set up a network of thirty-five hundred dispensaries, manned by constantly improving African

Part of the Lambaréné landscape

personnel, over a territory two-thirds as large as the United States. In less than a decade sleeping sickness has been conquered, leprosy brought under control, yellow fever eradicated, yaws practically eliminated. Recently a system of mobile X-ray trucks was inaugurated to aid in the fight against tuberculosis. Mobile teams already check every single inhabitant of the colony at least once a year. But great as this achievement may be, it can never aspire to bringing more than mass treatment and mass prevention. There will always be sickness which this system cannot reach. There will always be suffering which has to be met on the plane of direct human contact between healer and patient. There can never be enough hospitals of the Schweitzer type.

I have often heard the Hospital criticized for being not just old-fashioned, but anachronistic. It is indeed in many respects very old-fashioned and could not be otherwise. Even though it may no longer be true that Africans can feel at home only in bare and primitive surroundings, comfort and hygiene are still unknown in rural sections. After I had walked through a large number of African villages, the lack of hygiene and comfort at the Hospital did not seem incongruous. I saw many much better equipped hospitals in Equatorial Africa. I was shown modern government hospitals after having been told that they put the Schweitzer Hospital to shame. And, indeed, they had better buildings, cleaner wards, mosaic floors, and sometimes better equipment. The quality of the medicine practiced, however, was often incomparably poorer. In some of these hospitals the staff consisted of a single overworked doctor who, having to waste most of his time on useless paper work and statistics, was forced to leave treatment to incompetent orderlies. Often there was no doctor at all and a lonely, overburdened nurse had to try to diagnose and treat everything from toothache to leprosy. Intricate instruments, no longer in working order, were standing around; gleaming electrocardiographs or anesthesia machines had become corroded and irreparable after a short time in the equatorial humidity. Schweitzer's conservatism and his antipathy to gadgets became ever more justified from a practical point of view.

Schweitzer rejects modern man's belief in the redemption of the world by Things. With gadgetry kept at a minimum, the three hundred fifty beds are constantly occupied, the Leper Village filled to capacity. The need is so great that all theories about the Hospital's efficiency are irrelevant. For forty-five years the Hospital has fulfilled its function and has been a blessing to the whole region. It still is. This does not mean that improvements are not needed. They may be overdue. But day in, day out, patients emerge from the forest carried on the backs of their relatives or are delivered by pirogue or motorboat from hundreds of miles up or downstream. Often they are desperate cases, too ill to be saved. But they come here as a last resort and their families who left everything behind in order to seek help, know they will be received without being asked for money they do not possess, and will never be sent away. They know it, but they do not understand it. They cannot understand that the doctors and nurses who are caring for them receive no pay but room and board. To the African this seems impossible and he does not trust this aspect of the Hospital. Somehow, he thinks, these white people must be making a lot of money out of him. How, of course, is a mystery. But that anyone should give his services freely does not enter his head, because the African is very commercial-minded and expects a quid pro quo for every service. His witch doctors after all require prompt payment.

Since the patient is usually accompanied by half his family and, of course, food cannot be brought along for a protracted stay, the family has to be put to work in order to earn the food which is distributed to them. All the washing, scrubbing, planting, darning, ironing is done by ambulatory patients and their relatives. This causes a lot of grumbling for it is not quite clear—probably because it cannot really be explained to each individual through sheer lack of time—why they should have to work. Sometimes mild sabotage takes place and the women who are sent on an expedition to gather firewood will come back with symbolical little bundles of useless sticks. Then you hear shouting and palavers on all sides, because there is not enough wood for the outside hearth where instruments are sterilized and water distilled. All this constant activity is a visual delight. Men pick grapefruit or take care of the goats and the chicken yard. There are shoemakers at work, tailors, and even sculptors who carve again and again the typical ivory or ebony elephant which Schweitzer gives as a memento to appreciated visitors. Women carry buckets of water from the river to irrigate the truck gardens where their men till the soil. They launder the operating room linen near the generator shed, and do their own washing in the river.

They carry manioc leaves from the nearby field for the antelopes, while their men paddle flat-bottomed boats to the airstrip to fetch medical supplies.

Could you call waiting an activity? At this Hospital it is. People are always waiting. They hang around on benches in front of the Pharmacie, they sit on the stone steps at the nursery with babies in their arms. They wait for kerosene distribution, for food rations. They wait on stretchers in front of the operating room in order to be cut open. The most typical activity at this Hospital is to wait graciously and quietly—to wait for treatment, to wait for drugs, to wait for health. The African's time is not our time. Who cares about age?—About a wasted hour, day, or week? Patients stay for a month just wait-

To wait for treatment, to wait for drugs

ing for treatment. In the confusion of the waiting crowds they may have been overlooked or overlooked themselves —just forgot to show up for medicaments or examinations. Then through pain, one day they will remember and stand there, reproachfully showing the parts of their bodies which ache or refuse to function.

Women come to the Hospital to give birth. They are often so anemic that their hemoglobin has dropped to one-tenth of normal. No white woman would survive the delivery. But the Africans do. Their vitality is unbelievable. Rarely do they suffer from a single illness. The average patient at the Hospital is affected by four or five separate diseases. His fantastic African vitality struggles against the onslaught until one day the unequal fight is finished. The diseases win the battle and the patient lies down to die. His dying is part of his living, not an epilogue.

"They die more naturally than we do," said Father d'Espierres, the old missionary in the Congo. "They don't struggle so hard. There rarely is the agony of the white man who holds on to his individual life. Their spiritualism helps them also to accept death more naturally."

But the task of the Hospital is not to help patients to die. A desperate fight is waged to keep men and women alive.

Every patient has a cardboard label which he carries as an identity card. On it are written his name and a short description of the long list of his various disorders. Nearly all patients are anemic, often critically so. More than ninety per cent of the population is infected with venereal disease, especially gonorrhea. Although gonorrhea can indeed be treated by antibiotics, mass treatment has failed. The sexual mores of the people of Central Africa make effective treatment almost impossible. There is a great measure of sexual freedom which almost guarantees re-infection shortly after a cure has been obtained. All known antibiotics have been given successfully at first, then the microbes become resistant and the drug loses its effect. All patients have as another item on their label one or more of the innumerable types of worm infection, lingering on from childhood. Treatment can be effective here also, but re-infection is very hard to avoid because of eating habits and lack of hygiene. These infections are sufficient to cause the severe anemias which are so common. Then there may be leprosy or yaws, or both. And very often tuberculosis.

The patients who are brought in for emergency sur-

The operating room

gery or a delivery are likely to have a combination of all these horrors, but must often be taken immediately to the operating room for their fractures, hernias, or labor. The doctors are well aware of the risks they are taking. There is no choice. The opportunity to prepare the patient for major surgery by improving his condition is rare. The greatest chances simply have to be taken. Considering all these handicaps, mortality is surprisingly low. Is it because of that utter confidence of the patients which conscientious doctors often find embarrassing? Or because of a fantastic vitality which makes these people survive infernal combinations of illnesses which would kill us in a short time?

One fairy tale says that Africans never get cancer: I have seen many inoperable ones. Africans have all the diseases seen in Europe and America plus those peculiar to the tropics. Another fairy tale tells that they are less sensitive to pain. It is not true. They have greater fortitude in the face of pain as well as of death. But they are as sensitive as the most sensitive among us. If self-control is an indication of cultural level, the level here is high for they show unbelievable stoicism once they decide to be treated. In the dental chair I see the reaction of pain in their eyes. Unfortunately I always feel pain when I am inflicting it—a professional flaw. I have felt their pain often. But I have also felt an almost universal absence of that hysterical fear which in Western people so often intensifies and magnifies slight discomfort. The children were not afraid either. Maybe they felt that from the start I loved these African children with their enormous trusting eyes. Those who comfort themselves with the belief that Africans have lower human potentialities than we have, let them come and look at the children. How these children react to being accepted by you, how they love you, how they charm you with their little spontaneous gifts of an egg or a bunch of wild flowers! Illness, poverty, lack of opportunity may stunt their later lives. No doubt a girl of fifteen with two babies has less opportunity for continued mental growth than our high school girl. Heavy responsibilities come earlier in their lives than in ours and limit their development. But these are environmental factors, not intrinsic ones. I have never seen children who were less vandalistic. They seem to lack the aggressive games we are used to. But they breathe security. I have often marveled at the surprising sweetness, the lack of aggression in these children, their quiet, contented playfulness. A good explanation may be that they are breast-fed until they quite naturally abandon the breast. At the age of four or eight, or even as twelve-year-olds, they are never rejected. In the bosom of the mother quite literally, in the bosom of their clan a little more metaphorically, they grow up in security. Is it this which makes them later so confident in life—a life to be lived naturally, free of artificial pressures?

One thing is very baffling: living conditions which we simply assume to be absolute minimum requirements for human life turn out to be anything but conditions sine qua non. Human life can assume innumerable different patterns, all of them equally satisfactory, equally valid, equally human, and equally dignified. Yet, the form of African life one finds now in the forests or the savannahs is only a degenerated form of African life.

During the Middle Ages, African social organization was not inferior to its European equivalent. If anything, it was more democratic. Afterward, our system of inter-communal exchange developed rapidly, while theirs remained stagnant. Then followed the centuries during which the slave trade undermined their entire social structure and set tribe against tribe. Africans started to sell one another into slavery. Colonial exploitation followed and further disrupted the autochthonous cultures. Perhaps the last and most devastating step was an arbitrary, purely utilitarian system of education which neglected the firm basis of tribal integration. Then recently came urbanization. Uprooted individuals, unprepared for sudden estrangement from the protection of their clans, were transformed into a rebellious, unhappy "city-proletariat," apt to think of the white man only as the enemy he has so often proven to be, sometimes by malice but mostly by ignorance.

Is it too late to establish a purely human approach to problems of black Africa? It may be. Yet it is worth trying. Schweitzer is one who tried. And many of the people who work with him have established such close contacts that they are endeared to the Africans of the region. They came here to work for six months and stayed for years. They established a relationship on the only basis which is permanent: from person to person, from heart to heart. Most of our hasty methods of "aid" and "granting of independence" are barely camouflaged fear and selfishness. The beneficiaries feel this. The other method is slow, perhaps too slow, but then it is because we started so late. The loss is ours . . . and theirs.

The Grand Docteur will live on as the man in whom the Western conscience became incarnate long before it was exploited in order to adorn a political holding action in black Africa.

But I did not come to Lambaréné to write a dissertation on African politics. I came to work and to draw. Yet some of the innumerable impressions of native life have to be drawn in words.

Palavers for instance.

Palaver, palaver—the word most often repeated in Central Africa. What is a palaver? A discussion, a dispute, a semijuridical procedure, a quarrel. There are palavers about division of work, about distribution of food, about housing and accommodation, about tasks neglected. There are palavers about land, goats, and other possessions. And, of course, most palavers are somehow or other about women. But these quarrels are rarely explosive or even inflammable. They are just ever-present.

Most of the tribes of the Gabon region have a matriarchal social organization. The authority in the family is not the husband but the wife's oldest uncle. When children are born, it is this maternal uncle who takes charge. If the newborn child is a girl, the rejoicing is not purely emotional; a valuable piece of capital has been added to the family. For girls eventually become women who work and bear children and can be sold into marriage. The title to the girl is held by the oldest maternal uncle. He is free to sell his title at the appropriate time and for a fair price. Once the price has been paid, the buyer has the right to take possession without protest from the original titleholder. However this gentleman may be quite unco-operative in securing the girl for the buyer. That is the latter's worry!

The sales contract is in fact a three-way contract in which the seller and the buyer and also—to complicate matters—the merchandise has a say. If the merchandise hides, refuses to perform, or walks out, it is only fair that the seller make a refund. Unfortunately he is usually out of cash at the moment and a palaver starts which may keep a few generations interestingly occupied. Native judges, or arbiters, are consulted and the scales of justice are tipped to one side or the other depending on the bribes offered to the arbiter. There is an absolute passion for palavers of this and any other kind which take up much African mental energy. It is comforting to know that woman trouble is at least as endemic in Africa as it is in New York or Paris; it only assumes different aspects. Crimes of passion are rare, for the fires of passion are easily banked or quenched. The wages of sin are not death or the divorce court, but rather proper compensation in money or goats. After all, if you have bought your woman for hard-earned cash you have a right to demand remuneration if she is temporarily busy elsewhere.

The idea of romantic love has not yet been discovered here, probably because there has never been a black Tristan and Isolde. One does not marry a woman for her beauty but for her usefulness. She has to be a strong worker; traditionally the woman tills the land. As life-giver she is the one most qualified to propitiate the life-giving earth. She is the bearer of children; no one would marry a virgin of whom it is unknown whether she can bear many and healthy children. Premarital children usually have an assortment of fathers and are received in the maternal clan where they can grow up in security. Woman's defense against unfair male exploitation is a return to the maternal clan, taking her children along. A man may have multiple wives. It is purely a matter of economics, for sexual gratification is available outside the family quite easily and without feelings of guilt.

The body is accepted, it is accepted in its youthfulness and desire, and through it life fulfills itself. When it is old, it no longer adorns itself to pretend youthfulness. Its rhythm is nature's rhythm.

The young female body is frankly seductive, as nature wills it. It ornaments itself with colorful cloths and beads. Later it becomes motherly and is given over to the functions of raising children and working the earth. In old age, flabby breasts are not hidden, nor shrunken lips painted; wise grandmothers gravely stir their cooking pots and watch their granddaughters grow into women.

Often old couples came to my clinic comforting each other, showing their mutual concern with touching tenderness. Something deeply personal and intimate had survived all the desire and promiscuity, the childbearing and work. They had reached that human wisdom which does not depend on learning or knowledge.

Nominally the people of Gabon are Christians, Protestants or Catholics or both—"one never knows"—with much of the original animism surviving—"better be sure."

They accept Western medicine, often only after native medicines have proven themselves ineffective. Little is known about native medicine except that whatever there was is in decay. The theoretical basis, of course, was never biochemical, but magical. Nevertheless there were and are effective medicines, magically applied but empirically arrived at. How long, one might be tempted to ask, does the magical effectiveness of our own medicines last?

It has always been difficult to learn about native medicines, for they were kept secret by the witch doctors. The old witch doctors now take their prescriptions with them into their graves rather than divulge them to unworthy young ones who will buy penicillin and terramycin over the counter in the local general store and improvise their own medication or go to the hospitals of the whites for treatment. Yet even on the grounds of our Hospital I saw witch doctors. An orderly who became sick and did not react fast enough to the drugs given had his skin incised in magic patterns by a witch doctor and native medicine rubbed into the incisions. For the patient is apt to play it safe in this respect too. He takes both the traditional magical medicine and that of the whites. He may at the same time have himself treated at the Hospital one day, the next day at the government hospital a few miles downstream, and the third day by the *feticheur*, sometimes getting quickly killed by the combination, or by native medicine alone.

A child was brought in with spasm of the larynx. This tall three-year-old boy had been given an overdose of some indigenous medicine and all later medication, tracheotomy and so on, could not save the boy. He

Witch doctor and his patient

breathed a while and then suddenly his heart stopped. This was a case of involuntary poisoning, but intentional poisoning is common too. It is the most usual form of revenge. A woman was brought in with what looked like tetanus, but actually she had been poisoned in some local feud. The antidotes to these mysterious poisons are unknown to white doctors, but the African poisoners know them; there are cases where people were provisionally poisoned and given the choice between either giving in or dying. If the victim would see reason the antidote was administered. An effective warning!

The effects of native medicines often complicate the diagnosis of a disease, obscuring or perverting already complex symptoms. The hypothesis that a disease is caused by poison is sometimes a subterfuge in a case where no diagnosis can be made. It is an easy subterfuge because the naïve African believes, as do most other primitive people, that disease and death are caused by malevolence, be it poison or magic. In our own history it is only a short while ago that we burnt witches for similar reasons.

However, even if a diagnosis of "poisoning" is made it is not divulged, for one such proved poisoning can set an epidemic of revenge poisonings into motion. One day an old man was brought in with very high fever. Traces of native medicine were found in his mouth. He was obviously dying and much too irrational to answer questions. The autopsy showed him to have suffered from a combination of advanced tuberculosis, cirrhosis of the liver, syphilis, and an amoebic liver abscess. The immediate cause of death might have been the great quantity of woody fiber—probably some medicinal root given by a witch doctor—found in his intestines. His relatives, however, had made the diagnosis of poisoning.

The secret of indigenous medicines is a dangerous knowledge. A maid in the territory had betrayed an effective herb to her white mistress. A few days later the girl was found dead from poison.

A man cuts himself. A few hours later, in this climate, severe infection sets in. Two weeks afterward he arrives by pirogue at the Hospital with a gangrenous arm.

At lumber camps accidents occur every day. Compound fractures are brought in daily by pirogue, sometimes after a three-day trip under the hot sun on the river. The exhausted patient has to be operated on immediately.

A boy of thirteen was hit on the head by a falling branch. The brain lay bare. He was operated on and lives. Schweitzer was proud of Dr. Catchpool's handling of the case.

The New Ward especially is always filled with accident cases. I often visited it at night: rough wooden beds; patients with bandaged legs, arms, and heads; patients with huge ulcers; accident victims in plaster casts; a wife dozing against the footboard of her husband's bed; a mother sleeping on the floor under her son's cot.

Back in the Ward some people sit around an oil lamp, frying fish over a little chip fire on the stone floor, and sharing it with the man whose leg won't heal because he has only twenty per cent hemoglobin and a barking, suspicious cough. Nearby, on the special bed constructed

Special bed for paralyzed patient

by Dr. Catchpool from packing cases, lies the man with
the broken spine. The bed hangs from pulleys so the
partially paralyzed patient can move without help.

The Ward at night at first looks like an inferno of
smoke, suffering, and stench. Then gradually you notice
how full it is of bubbling good humor, friendliness, and
mutual sympathy. People otherwise lost are being healed.

"What do you think of this Hospital?" I asked a
bright-looking young mechanic from Libreville whose
foot had been crushed by a tractor. He is the boy who
constantly asked me about New York and read whatever
he could find.

"*Eh bien,*" he said, "the treatment could not be finer
and the doctors are better than in any other place, but of
course the accommodation is terrible."

I believe this sums up neatly Young Africa's view of the Hospital.

Because of the easy rapport I established with people of the various tribes, I found their intertribal relationships all the more puzzling. For them, people from another tribe have little claim to sympathy. The good Samaritan is only conceivable if you are a Samaritan yourself. There is no concept of universal human brotherhood. A man has fallen out of a palm tree. If he is from your tribe you carry him on your back to the next village. If he is not, you pass by and let him die. The Christian catechist who leads the evening prayer at the Hospital sleeps next to a totally helpless man who has come all alone from very far away and has no one to look after him. The nurses have been trying to persuade the good Christian to take a little care of his neighbor. But he will not; this fellow comes from another tribe, he is beyond the pale. Yet every night the catechist is fervently singing psalms with his followers.

There is no deliberate cruelty to animals. There is just no realization that they are living creatures with feelings. Children swing a bird around, a string tied to one of its legs. Is it so different from our children doing the same with a May bug? Torturing and killing for pleasure is savage in any color; in African jungles, at fox hunts, at the pheasant shoot. Savage is he who has not yet realized that any other living creature is as real as he is.

This applies to the position of women too. After all, you buy your wife and she becomes inevitably an object. This makes it difficult to accept white women in positions

of authority. That a woman can be your superior is still unimaginable to the African. But, after all, I know a few white men who also have difficulty in resigning themselves to such a situation.

To the woman doctor a patient answered: *"Oui, monsieur."*

She explained that she was not *monsieur,* but *doctoresse.* "Do you understand?"

"Oui, monsieur doctoresse!"

There are many stories about taboos. A girl to whom since birth manioc had been taboo came to the Catholic boarding school and was told by a nun at First Communion: "Now you are grown up, Marie. Show the devil you are no longer under his power." The girl conquered herself, ate a few spoonfuls of manioc, and dropped dead.

Dr. Schweitzer liked to tell the story of the lumber merchant with a glass eye who had to go to Brazzaville for a few days. He left his glass eye on his desk and said to his men, "My eye will watch you and tell me who did not work." When he came back from Brazza the normal amount of work had been done. The lumber merchant rubbed his hands and a month later took off to Libreville for a few days, taking care to leave his eye on the desk again. When he returned not a stitch of work had been done. At first he did not find his eye either. It was on his desk all right, but someone had covered it with an old hat.

There is a contra-magic for every magic!

At times an African woman goes into a frightful tantrum for mysterious reasons. She sees ghosts and in utter fright rolls herself screaming through the dust. I saw such a case but cannot describe it. The very sight stiffens one

with horror. Sedatives do not work. A witch doctor might. For instance, by shaving a spot the size of a quarter on the woman's head the possessing spirit is given a chance to get out and the woman becomes calm. In some cases even the witch doctor is powerless. The district doctor of Lambaréné, however, then lives his hour of triumph: he gives the woman an injection of sugar-water and at once the attack stops.

"Often," he explained, "the tantrums are brought on by an abnormally low blood sugar. These people have such irregular eating habits you see, they'll gorge themselves on Monday and have nothing more to eat until Thursday. After I discovered this drop in the blood sugar I followed the sugar-water practice. It is one of the few instances in which I can beat my colleague, the witch doctor!"

One day there was panic in the Leper Village. A mysterious stranger had been seen trying to stab people through the bamboo walls of the huts at night. Trudi did her own detective work. She found the man and took him firmly by the hand. The murderer was so surprised at her lack of fear that he followed her meekly and was locked up. Later his special pirogue was found. It was very narrow, very flat, and very fast so that it could shoot through the narrowest, shallowest jungle streams. The prisoner belonged to a gang of seven "leopard-men" who murder a victim, cut him up, and sell fragments of the body as fetishes. The police came to fetch him quietly. Politically it is not expedient to give much publicity to these anachronisms!

A few times each day a child is born on the other

side of the thin partition separating my clinic from the Delivery Room. The young mother lies exhausted on the hard delivery table with a tiny black baby in her arms. Around the table women are dancing a strange African dance, half obscene, half religious. In the room hangs that specific African smell, part human, part elephant. The grandmother dances first. With legs apart, arms raised, belly rhythmically revolving. She smiles gravely in ecstatic happiness. Behind her dance the sisters and aunts. Men are not present. The singing is monotonous and obsessive. The women look at each other from the corners of their eyes as if in mutual understanding: something collective has happened, something concerning all of them. They seem to flirt with one another, stamping their feet, turning their bellies, raising their hands, sing-songing. The mother's eyes see nothing but the baby in her arms.

On my way to my room after work one night, I saw that the baby with tetanus in Nurse Almut's room must be dying at last. Almut had been up with the child for three nights. In front of her door the father was sitting with his brothers and some children. They didn't cry, they just looked exhausted.

"Is it your only child?" I asked.

"No," he said, "I have other children, but it hurts just the same."

"Life is hard," I said helplessly.

"It is terrible," the black man said.

From my window I saw the mother. Her hands rose and fell rhythmically. She was all alone, fighting against some god or demon for the life of her child. She was slight and cross-eyed. The short poor cotton dress hung around her spindly legs. Suddenly she stopped her sing-songing. There was a commotion in Almut's room. A few moments later I followed a little procession: the father and mother and the children walking down the steps to the river with their belongings. One child carefully carried the small bundle that was the baby. Wailing softly, they climbed into their pirogue to take the dead child to their village up the river.

The doctor was leaning against Almut's door. "God damn it," he swore. His face looked gray and he lighted his fifteenth cigarette. "C'mon Almut," he said, "let's have a look at the meningitis child. I'll never get used to it." Death was always with us there, like all the other basic ingredients of living.

Through the jungle to the grave

There was the man with the lung abscess. For weeks they had been tapping his chest. Every day I saw him climb onto the table to have the monstrous syringe stuck in. A pint one day, a quart the next, a pint and a half the third. The man walked to the table on his stick, his face already quiet as in death yet marked with the suffering that still is life. He was unaccompanied by relatives, completely alone. One morning very quietly and resignedly he suddenly lay still. There was no one to take him back to his village. No eight-day tom-tom for him, no dirge by torchlight. His body was wrapped in palm leaves, a neat parcel of man, and placed on a stretcher. Two strong stretcher-bearers carried the body through the jungle to the grave. In front walked Jean, the orderly, with long vine ropes; behind, a frightened boy carried a pick and shovel. Then followed a white nurse, Toni, with her Bible.

You can call it a mass grave. But that reminds one of Buchenwald. It is impossible to dig individual graves in the hard, stony subsoil of the jungle. The grave was a raw rectangular hole, cut in the red, stony earth under the palm trees. The body was lowered and Toni read a prayer. Then the earth was shoveled back until the body was quite covered. The quiet was absolute, even the palms did not move. The dead man was already in communion with the other dead. The living worked in silence, then walked back, carrying the rope, the stretcher, the pick, and the shovel.

Night was falling rapidly. I went to my room to write until midnight. Before going to bed I looked out. Lights were moving up the riverbank. What could it be?

I took my kerosene lamp and found my way to the river. A woman in advanced pregnancy was climbing up the bank. She carried a basket on her head. A second woman carried a huge semicircular basket on her arm. Both giggled. More were coming, for I heard paddles in the water.

"Did you go fishing?" I asked.

They giggled again. "Of course we went fishing. We go fishing every night."

"Are they allowed to get out of their beds?" I asked the old nurse the next day.

She grinned. Obviously I was a newcomer. "Nothing to allow, they just go. We can't have cops around here. It would not help anyway."

"I also heard a motorboat at the landing," I said, "around midnight."

"Not surprised," said the old nurse. "The other day one of our lady patients was visited by a delegation of twenty-five men from her village in the middle of the night!"

"Did they stay here overnight?" I asked.

"Don't ask silly questions!" she answered severely.

And so in the isolated community of Lambaréné I witnessed life and death in all their modes as intensely as in that frequently styled "hub of the world"—New York.

Animals in the Landscape

Some intellectuals like to tell you that Schweitzer loves the animals a great deal more than the humans in his jungle empire. But then, intellectuals like to theorize, and all the long distance psychologizing about Schweitzer proved to be completely false. From a distance of many thousands of miles his relationship to animals may seem sentimental. From close by you see that it is an impartial and somewhat detached lovingness. He gets totally involved the moment he sees a suffering creature, whatever that creature may be. After careful observation I came to the conclusion that he loves life, animals and people equally well.

You see him feeding chickens from a little bag of rice
he always carries and suddenly he may give a hen, showing too obvious signs of free enterprise and rugged indi-
vidualism, a good hard kick in the pants.

He will go to great lengths in order not to torture or
kill animals unnecessarily, and will put a caterpillar carefully on a leaf instead of crushing it under his foot. But
finding a nest of touchingly naked baby rats in a box
which ought to contain aspirin, he will have them destroyed, though not without regret. He will take the lead
when a dangerous snake is discovered in a tree practically
overhanging the Pharmacie, and the three-yard-long animal is beaten to death. He is no fool; he has mosquitoes
and tsetse flies killed, for he realizes that in the combat
against disease trillions of microbes have to be sacrificed
for human life. His Reverence for Life which, as I see it,
has—consciously or unconsciously—its origin in a profound nature mysticism, is tempered with good sense. No
vegetarianism is practiced at Lambaréné because the
limits of reverence for other expressions of life are dic-
tated not by arbitrary evaluations of lower forms of life,
such as plants, and the higher life of animals, but by
purely practical considerations. No life is valued above
any other.

Innumerable forms swarm over Lambaréné. Wild
birds, such as the little bright yellow-and-black ones
called "gendarmes," adorn the trees with the glitter of
jewels. Their round nests look like fruits, and hundreds
of these fruits hang in a single palm, chosen for some
unknown reason, until the tree dies. Then the gendarmes
descend on another palm.

Metallic, tiny hummingbirds suck honey from orange flowers. Ever-present, nearly colorless lizards shoot like lightning along walls and ceilings, hunting for insects. One almost transparent lizard appeared every afternoon at exactly four o'clock between the curtain and the mosquito screen of my clinic, looking for some big fly which invariably kept the rendezvous. There were occasionally little scorpions—not terribly dangerous—to be found around the washbasins; and lots of formidable looking spiders, who never did any harm. The African giant-versions of cockroaches and water bugs proved to be as exquisitely sensitive and knowing about the approach of the threatening human foot as their cousins in America. They actually laugh in your face when you spray them with DDT and quickly disappear between the planks of the floor or wall, after having feasted on the collar of your best nylon shirt which now shows a series of big holes.

There are hundreds of chickens, less stupid and much less domesticated, also less fat, than ours. They lay tiny eggs all over the place, making it a children's sport to find these eggs and offer them to you as valuable presents. The chickens are not "chicken" at all, but will attack even big cats who come too close to their chicks. They are the terror of small snakes, which they kill with flawless technique. The roosters parade all over in their brilliant colors. Their perverted sense of timing makes them a kind of round-the-clock wake-you-up service. They were originally brought here by patients as currency and so were the ducks, hundreds of them. Even these black-and-white birds with berry-like red protrusions around the eyes look quite wild. They are aggressive and independent and constantly surrounded by multitudes of charming yellow-and-black ducklings, fluffs of wool which seem to aim at becoming ordinary Long Island ducks, but turn inevitably into these big, black, fierce-eyed African monsters. Their keeper is a tiny, emaciated, and very childish little man. But the chief of the poultry yard is a sweet-tempered ex-leper who looks like a huge Frankenstein monster and has one of the finest smiles I have ever seen in a human being.

Among the domesticated birds lives a toucan called Jackie. He may not be a real toucan because this species seems to be limited to South America, but let's call him an African toucan since this is not a textbook on zoology.

The toucan called Jackie

Jackie has a human eye behind his monstrous beak. He likes to land on your shoulder, loves to be talked to, begs for a banana, and has a distinct range of expressions in his beady eye from "Why don't you stroke my throat?" to "Now you are a real dear!" after you have performed this function.

To me the least sympathetic among the animals is the chimpanzee Fritzli. His constant and aimless jumping around, swinging from branches, destroying boxes, grabbing legs, pulling goats' tails, reminds me too much of life in New York. The way he hangs on the shoulder of Mamba, the leper who is his keeper and who looks exactly like him after many years of nearly married life, recalls too clearly the way my fellow chimps swing with me from straps in the subway. The little white-nosed monkey, sitting quietly behind the barracks of the orderlies, playing amiably with goats and children, has much more charm. Actually, Fritzli is rapidly getting too big to stay here. He is nearly four years old and soon he will have to go to a permanent home in the Bern zoo, where he will have less opportunity of biting the hand that feeds him or pulling the leg innocently passing by.

Whenever you look on the ground or the floor you see something crawling—usually ants. There are many kinds of ants in Africa, from the most horrifying to the most innocent. Size does not have very much to do with the degree of ferocity. There are tiny ones which bite most irritatingly, large ones which walk over you without a second look, and still larger ones with claws like miniature lobsters who would rather give up claws and head than release their grip. A classical African ordeal used to be (and in Africa you are never too sure exactly where the border between "used to be" and "is" lies) the exposure of one's victim to these ants. It was a slow but not painless demise.

Horrible stories are told everywhere about invasions staged by indeflectible armies of ants. In the Congo a man told me of waking up in the middle of the night and seeing himself surrounded by ants. His only way of escape was to grab his kerosene lamp, spread a circle of kerosene around him, and by slowly expanding it escape from the insects. Kerosene seems to be one of the few defenses against them. Another Belgian I met had just rescued his baby from an invasion of carnivorous ants, which had already covered the child completely. Although badly bitten, the baby survived.

One has the impression that people are more afraid of attacks by ants than by all the other animals combined. One night in Lambaréné an ant army was deflected— also by kerosene barrage—from its march toward the chicken yard. On a previous occasion all chickens had completely vanished after the army had marched through. Not only chickens vanish. A local administrator in the Belgian Congo, when it came to the inevitable topic of ants, told me how his predecessor once had to keep a prisoner overnight. Prisons are not easily built in the forest and the few real prisons I saw were rather open structures where the inmates seemed to have a fairly good time. They went to the movies at night and returned docilely because there is no place where one has to work less and is better fed. The story goes that the prison director of Port-Gentil received from his superior during the war the order to halve the inmates' rations. He wired back, "Impossible." A new telegram with the peremptory question "Why impossible?" was answered by the director in these words, "Inmates would leave."

However, back to the *brousse* administrator who accepted delivery of a murderer after sunset. Since there are no Black Marias, prisoners are transported in a net-like cage made of vines. The official gave the prisoner his supper and left him for the night in his cage next to the administration hut where he was to be interrogated in the morning. During the night the administrator once woke up. He thought he heard some shouting from where the prisoner was parked, but did not pay much attention. After all, prisoners often shout. And so he went back to sleep. When in the morning he went to take a look at the fellow, there was no fellow left, just a clean skeleton.

Enough about ants? Just one word more. King Solomon advised us to go to the ant and become wise. He probably had in mind the variety of ants Dr. Schweitzer entertains on his writing table.

For some years he has been watching this particular family of ants, a few hundred or a few thousand quite benign and harmless ones, which live in a nest somewhere under the floor boards of his room. After every meal he puts a little piece of fish under the kerosene lamp on his table; immediately the ants crawl up the table leg, walk in a neat line across the top piled with papers, and start to tackle the fish offering from all sides. It requires five or six of the tiny insects to transport a huge fragment of two cubic millimeters of fish across the table, down the leg to their residence. Dr. Schweitzer and I watched with de-

Dr. Schweitzer entertains his ants

light how first the softer pieces of fish were chosen in preference to older, harder ones.

I am not yet through with animal life at the Hospital. Among the birds in residence are a number of pelicans, one of which, Parsifal, was found shot during my stay. X-rayed and found full of pellets he lingered on for two weeks, was given terramycin and fed with fish, but died at last all the same.

"How stupid," exclaimed Schweitzer, "to shoot my poor bird! A stranger must have done it, for people around here know my pelicans and they would think twice before shooting them." He was again entirely involved; treated and nursed the bird himself and was full of interest when after its death a young doctor performed an autopsy and explained the lethal factors. Again, full devotion, but no sentimentality.

I myself was responsible for the rescue and protective custody of a big hoot owl caught napping in the afternoon sun by some of the leper children. The formidable claws were cruelly tied together and the owl could hardly keep his eyes open, which gave him an expression of deep philosophical resignation. The children were never deliberately cruel but simply unaware of the fact that an owl does not enjoy being swung around on a rope. In procession we went to present the owl to the Grand Docteur, since liberating the animal with its clipped wings would have been as cruel as leaving it to the children. The owl now lives in the cage where Parsifal died, is well-fed, and enjoys his undisturbed meditations and his view of the chicken yard.

An eagle also had been caught in the Leper Village.

I found him lying prostrate in an abandoned hut, the enormous beak dug into the mud floor, the fierce eyes staring into mine. I could not save him because eagles cooked with manioc make an excellent soup, and the villagers did not want to change their menu.

Of gorillas I saw only one oversized skull, given to me in payment for a root canal filling by a missionary who had shot the big animal some years before. I was just unlucky, if you can call it that, for gorillas abound here. In some parts of the forest the natives simply refuse to accompany you a step farther, because this territory belongs to "Monsieur," as the gorilla is usually called. He lives happily enough with wife and children in the bush, (he even constructs chairs to sit on), and enjoys life quite peacefully as long as he is not disturbed. He resents encroachment on his privacy, but even if incommoded he is not really murderous. The gorilla seems to be of a more monogamous disposition than most of his human cousins in Africa and elsewhere. He might take your intrusion for an attempt to seduce his wife. The etiquette on meeting a gorilla is: 1) stand stockstill; 2) look the gorilla firmly but not unkindly in the eye; 3) start to retreat, walking backward slowly (provided of course that there is not another gorilla standing behind you!). You will escape unscathed. But even if you should advance, the gorilla will not kill you. He may only crush you a bit, break some bones, and almost certainly scalp you. But as soon as he is sure that you are no longer a potential danger he'll leave you alone to die all by yourself, except when you are lucky enough to be picked up by one of your clansmen and be brought to the Hospital, like the man I saw there. He had escaped with merely a crushed leg.

Chimpanzees usually don't attack, but make such a nerve-scattering noise with their constant chatter that on one occasion Dr. Schweitzer, concentrating on directing a construction project, ordered his men to send all those chattering women and children behind him back to the village. It was politely pointed out that if he would turn around he would see not women and children but a large family of chimps.

There are many horror stories about crocodiles, but the only one I can tell from personal experience is purely culinary. My crocodile was very old, very tough, and covered with a brown sauce. Humans here seem to find crocodiles more appetizing than the other way around and the Ogowe crocodile hardly ever eats a human being.

A crocodile for dinner

He might express his resentment by nipping off an arm or leg, but he despises the rest of us.

Much more dangerous than the crocodiles are the hippos, whose jolly rotundity gives a wrong idea of their active and resentful little brains. They hate to be disturbed by the slow and ponderous little motorboats which scrape their backs as they are peacefully snoring, enjoying a siesta on the bottom of a shallow river. Then they become quite excited and mad, start to gallop after the motorboats, which have often capsized or been left to sink with big gashes in their hulls. Hippos have formidable tusks. Once, at table, a fat government bigwig told how he and his crew had been pursued onto the banks by a herd of hippos which, as he said, "made the blacks climb into the nearest trees!" He tried to create the illusion that he himself had subdued the hippos by singing the "Marseillaise" and waving the tricolor at them, but after he left it was whispered that he had implored the "blacks" to haul him into a tree as fast as they could.

Leopards have retreated to the deepest part of the jungle and are rigorously protected in order not to become extinct. The few expensive skins I saw in Kano had probably been imported from Seventh Avenue.

Elephants and snakes are the only remaining animals around Lambaréné worth mentioning. As I already stated regretfully, the closest I came to an elephant was when I stepped into his excrement a few miles from the Hospital. The African elephant is quite elusive and incalculable and only after considerable effort have some of them been tamed by the Belgians on the equator, where they are put to work hauling lumber. But even they are now being re-

placed by an American machine called the *catère-pillare*.
I studied the physiognomy of a few African elephants in
the small zoo at Leopoldville where they are cruelly
chained to concrete by their legs. They look even more
anachronistic than their Indian cousins, but are much
more mobile around the ears, which, like enormous flaps
of chamois, constantly register fast fluctuations in mood.

Around Lambaréné everybody pretends to have shot
a few elephants and proudly tells you how dangerous it
is, especially if you hunt the small fierce kind which
abounds some three miles from the Hospital, but eluded
me so successfully. I was offered, in payment for services,
about eight molars and a little tusk. My patients seemed
to believe that anything dental was of particular interest
to me. I asked for details about the temper of these elephants and was told that, like all other animals of the
jungle, they have sufficient insight into the blackness of
the human heart to prefer, by far, staying out of our way.
Only sometimes they run amuck and flatten an entire
plantation or village in a single night. Supposedly this
usually happens after they have eaten some semipoisonous
plants which have a maddening effect. I myself saw one
plantation ravaged, with all the young trees trampled into
something that looked like a health salad.

Apparently elephants do not believe in "together-
ness." The males, having to ponder grave questions of
life and death for the whole herd, do not wish to be disturbed by the chatter of wives and the trumpeting of
children. They therefore mostly keep to themselves and
it is whispered that this is the secret of their longevity.

Snakes of all kinds are plentiful. It is safe to assume

that any snake you meet is poisonous. Boa constrictors, of course, are not. They are often found extremely well-fed and fast asleep, after swallowing a whole goat or a dog. At Lambaréné such a boa was once found, and the dog which emerged from it, after the snake was halved, is reported to have walked away solemnly wagging his tail.

Africans would not dream of taking a walk in the jungle unless armed with a stout machete. I never did this because of my firm conviction that at the first appearance of a big snake I would drop the machete and run. One little patient at the Hospital was treated for hideous wounds in the buttocks. While he walked peacefully at his mother's hand over a jungle path, a boa had suddenly practiced its constriction act on him. The mother, obviously not inclined to drop her machete, succeeded in killing the boa, but unfortunately shredded her son's posterior in the process.

Cobras and other poisonous monsters also generally pay their compliment to man's greater venom by trying to disappear as soon as they hear his step. Most snake bites occur when people inadvertently step on a sleeping snake. As a precaution Schweitzer keeps the Hospital grounds as clean as possible. Undergrowth and grass is kept at a minimum and pineapple patches have been eliminated because snakes love to dwell under their umbrellas of leaves.

Some snakes are so faithful to a particular palm tree that they stay with it as it grows. Eventually the time comes when they can't get down any more and they live out their lives among the palm nuts and leaves, catching birds. There is a palm nut picker in Lambaréné who twice during his career had to defend himself against the same snake in the same tree.

Another precaution: don't steer your pirogue along the riverbank where branches overhang the water. Snakes like to slide down into the pirogue. It is one of their few chances to get down on what looks like solid earth, for most of them detest water. Snakes are caught, charmed, and even milked for poison. My patient, the famous charmer, usually carried one around as a pet.

On the other hand there are entire tribes of Africans who will not hunt crocodiles because of an ancient non-aggression pact closely observed by both parties.

Now to the domestic animals at the Hospital.

People have been shocked by the informality with which animals and humans mix, and although it is perhaps not always defensible on hygienic grounds, the mixture adds considerably to the charm of the place. The Hospital without the animals would perhaps be wiser but certainly much sadder!

The animal kingdom represented by ducks, chickens, goats, monkeys, pelicans, sheep, parrots, ants, and especially cats and dogs has, as far as I know, unlimited freedom within Schweitzer's domain except for a few rules of etiquette and a few taboos. These do not apply to his six or so antelopes, who live a somewhat pampered though segregated life, or to the two wild boars of whom Tecla, the best loved, has lately also been put reluctantly behind a fence. The antelopes can't be left to roam because they swiftly disappear into a bush life to which they are no longer adapted. Pigs simply behave just too

Dr. Schweitzer's antelopes

piggishly. They will lie down immovably in front of doors and drive a tusk into your leg if you try too energetically to move them.

About etiquette. You feed the animals whenever you feel like it, you can even pet them within limits but always with the back of your hand, because all these goats and dogs and cats visit sick wards teaming with microbial life of the most horrifying varieties, walk through grass through which lepers just waded, and are (if someone wanted to establish records) perhaps the greatest microbe carriers per square inch of body surface anywhere on earth. Each time my favorite cat, Minou, sat on my bed I tried to banish a picture of all the trillions of infectious bacilli, cocci, amoebae, and spirochetes from my mind, and stroked the sweet animal according to etiquette with the back of my hand, which of course a minute later I used to wipe the sweat out of my eyes.

Feeding animals from one's hand is taboo for good reason: a bite or scratch might well mean tetanus or blood poisoning. Fish is allowed for the carniverous ones, but meat scraps for cats and dogs are frowned upon because meat is such a rare commodity at the Hospital.

How about the goats? Aren't they eaten? There are hundreds of goats divided into two categories: the small hardy African goats called *cabris*—often given in payment for treatment by the patients—and the Nubian goats originally imported from America in a big publicity campaign. These poor animals were shipped from New Orleans, after traveling for many days through the United States in a big white truck proclaiming their destination in huge letters: "Milk Goats for Dr. Schweitzer." They carried a complete two months' supply of special food and were accompanied by their private American veterinarian. After having been smiled at by black and white alike they arrived in Lambaréné, where to the embarrassment of everyone, they gave a few drops of milk, then stopped. From month to month they looked more melancholy. They despised the Lambaréné greenery and lost weight. To the extent of their energy to propagate, they produced some anemic looking kids which after having looked around sadly invariably gave up the ghost. Yet the Nubians are somewhat sacred; they were given with so much generosity and had traveled so far around the globe that they cannot decently be eaten. Instead, they have become an additional burden on the nursing staff who treat them more or less like semiprivate patients.

Goats of the African variety are also rarely killed. I never found out in what way a goat had to transgress in order to end in the pot, but once in a while one finds a sauce over his rice with something animal in it and little bones and it is whispered that this is *cabri*. African goats are not eaten very much by Africans either. They form the African's capital, as do his women who nowadays are not eaten at all as far as I know. The goats are pampered more than the women and are similarly kept for bartering in those many palavers or semijuridical disputes which seem to keep Africans fascinated from generation to generation. In the latter situation they also act as currency. Wives are bought for a certain number of goats with

Goats form the African's capital

perhaps some cash thrown in as small change. They are eaten only, semiritualistically, on occasions of great solemnity, such as weddings, births, deaths, and similar festivities.

The Schweitzer goats, as far as I can see, have as their main vocation the production of dung. Theoretically, this should all be used for the fabulous truck gardens, but I have the impression that the lifework of the goat could be organized better, for as it is, most of the dung seems to collect between the heel and sole of one's shoes or spread evenly over the naked soles of the Africans, so that everybody is seen rhythmically scraping it off against planks, porches, and special scrape-irons at the entrance to the dining room. To me the most important way in which goats really earn their keep consists in their decorative function. Few things are more beautiful than to see them in the morning light stampeding from the enclosure when that great magician, the goatherd Maduma, releases them in the slanting rays of the sun; goats pink-and-beige, mouse-gray, and black, with their kids in all shades and sizes; dainty ewes and lecherous he-goats often with broken horns, mutilated in combat, their comic opera, Semitic noses stretched upward in a satanically obscene leer. Two distinct groups rush in opposite directions: one toward the gardens and the other always along the same path in single file, galloping down behind the Hospital. Before dark Maduma gathers them all as by magic in a quick roundup.

During the day goats are everywhere. As I awoke, I heard the tapping of little hoofs on the porch in front of my room and as I opened my door, they jumped away

into the ditch. I saw their wistful heads sticking out of
the tall grass wherever I went. At certain points between
the wards are large wooden boxes used as garbage cans
and in each box usually there were one or two of the billy
goats laughing maliciously at me when I passed by, while
chewing something indescribable. Under the sterilizing
plant, a primitive hearth in front of the Pharmacie, there
were always a number of them, rubbing their ribs against
the bricks, watching me with their yellow eyes. Between
the waiting patients two young kids trying out their
budding horns jumped up with their heads bent forward
and sideward, a split second later their skulls crashed
together; an eternal ballet with always the same chore-
ography.

Goats are prone to skin diseases and are then painted
with a purple antiseptic which makes the rotund and
older goats look embarrassingly like middle-aged provincial ladies with purple hair rinses.

Toward evening many of the goats gathered around
the guest rooms in the tall grass, sunning themselves and
ruminating before going back to their quarters. I usually
saw three or four matrons on the sloping roof opposite
my room, suckling their kids while enjoying the warmth
of the corrugated iron.

If I forgot to mention sheep, it is because African
sheep look exactly like goats, only a little more sheepish.

From goats to dogs is just a small step, for they like
to chase each other. The only thoroughbred, an elegant
German shepherd, Porto, was left here by a visiting oil
heiress and is affectionately called by Schweitzer the
"Petroleum Mutt." Porto has something of deer in him,

loves to frighten complacent, cud-chewing goats, scares them out of their wits, and teasingly challenges them to attack. He then acrobatically jumps over them and starts a flank attack until the herd disperses in despair. Porto is the sporting aristocrat of the dog world here.

Porto's antipode is the animal I called "Ugly" to which name he responded with as much tail-wagging and hindquarter-wiggling as to his original name. Ugly is roughly a fox terrier, but his curly tail, fat belly, bow legs, and earless head give him the shape of a Victorian teapot. That he has no ears is due to the skill of a visiting veterinarian who looked with great pity on the tropical ulcers on poor Ugly's ears and decided to amputate them on the theory that if you have no ears you can't have ulcers on them. So now Ugly has no ears but has ulcers where his ears used to be and many flies gather around his pitiful little head. Every day someone bandages his head and in the morning Ugly looks like a scientifically swathed teapot. Around noon he is chewing the bandage with great satisfaction and looks more pitiful although less ridiculous than ever. In any other place on earth Ugly would have been destroyed years ago, because "this is no life even for a dog." At Schweitzer's, Ugly survives, is loved by everybody, gets extra bits from the table, and positively smiles at you with his wholly indescribable face when he suspects you have a cookie in your pocket. Ugly is a tail-wagging argument against euthanasia.

There are some fifteen more mutts, the genetic scum of all the canine on earth. A disgruntled and unhappy black mixture called Hector was, I believe, the one who came here in a somewhat romantic manner. His boss, a decrepit white man from the brush, had been treated at the Hospital for a considerable time. One day he decided he had had enough, pronounced himself cured, and went back by pirogue to his place in the woods. For a year or so he was not heard from. Then one evening, under a full moon, a pirogue stopped at the Hospital, rowed by a few anxious Africans. One of them alerted the Hospital staff: When the doctors got to the landing they found the pirogue manned by two black oarsmen and, silhouetted against the moonlight, their former white patient with a few chickens on his lap, his meager belongings and his dog at his feet. The remarkable thing was that the white man sitting in the pirogue was dead.

Some people say the dog was Hector, others that it was Ugly. It does not matter, for every dog and every cat, every owl and every pelican is kept. More than that, every human being is kept too. Schweitzer never refuses shelter.

After meals, dogs sit in front of the dining room waiting for scraps. The tame goats join in for sociability, as do a number of cats.

Waiting for scraps

Before taking leave of the animal kingdom, there are three parrots, two of them rather inferior and quite inarticulate. They whistle beautifully but hardly speak a reasonable word. Externally they can scarcely be distinguished from the rhetorically much more gifted and highly regarded Kudeku. All three have a lovely silver-gray body which gets lighter and lighter toward the nearly white head, contrasting dramatically with the black beak. All three have red tail feathers. This is nothing special, for the parrots around here are most conformistic in shape and color. Whole flights of them converse in all languages in the palms between Hospital and Village and fly up like vulgar city pigeons when you clap your hands.

Kudeku never talks to your face. Patiently, with an aloof expression in his eyes, he lets you whistle or talk. As soon as you turn your back he imitates the theme you have whistled or says quietly: *"Bonjour, docteur,"* or *"Cochon!"* (Pig!) I wonder who taught him this insult?

In the beginning I thought it ludicrous that one could not meet a doctor, an air force general, a priest, or a housewife without the conversation turning to parrots. I never liked the silly animals. But people are lonely on the equator and these conversing birds are their solace. The priest told me of a parrot of his who was particularly stupid. After a full year he still did not speak a word, not even *"Bonjour, mon Père."* Very much distressed he greeted his parrot every morning with, *"Dis bonjour, imbécile!"* and gave him a light tap on his claws with a ruler. Time went by until the weekly airplane brought the Bishop on an inspection tour of his diocese. The Bishop looked at everything kindly, complimented our priest, and said, "What a nice parrot you have." Deeply touched, the parrot then spoke his first words, *"Dis bonjour, imbécile!"*

Schweitzer also had his story. One evening while writing he heard a chick squealing outside. "Hm," he said to himself, "the idiots forgot again to lock up the chicks." He opened his door, found no chick, and went on writing. But the squealing continued. After a while he looked around, again saw no chick, but only his parrot sitting on his perch looking quite innocent (here the Grand Docteur gave the ideal impersonation of a parrot looking innocent!), and went on writing. But the irritating squealing continued at intervals until Schweitzer finally realized that his parrot was kidding him!

The Protestant missionary sitting opposite—for all such stories are told during lunch—contributed one about his parrot. Once during a wedding ceremony in the Mission chapel, at the very second when the bridegroom, a fellow missionary, had to say "Yes," a distinct voice came as from Heaven saying, "Aren't you stupid!"

I once visited a doctor and his wife who had been in Africa a bit too long. They rarely spoke to each other directly, but almost exclusively via a couple of acrobatic parrots which lived in an artificial tree in their shabby living room. In order to express their mutual irritation they would take the animals on their wrists, feed them from their mouths, and chatter at them in insulting language with that particular strident tone of voice so characteristic of married couples who have long ago given up all hope of true communication. Only when the parrots started to swear back could man and wife smile at each other, sourly and desperately, while taking long sips of whisky.

Another couple I met in an isolated spot of the Congo, a highly conscientious local administrator and his young wife, also used to converse through their parrot, but lovingly, benevolently, and sadly. Their house was beautifully kept and their garden a paradise, cultivated with immense patience by the wife. Only later I heard how unhappy these people were, though not with each other —theirs seemed to be a deep human relationship—but they had an only child in Europe, incurably ill. They just could not bear the verbal transmission of their sadness.

Parrots fulfill a basic need

So parrots fulfill a basic need of lonely whites under the tropical sun in their often unbearable loneliness. They bring a bit of gaiety or act as safety valves for pent-up emotions and frustrations. They fulfill these functions exactly and well because they are unpredictable, register conversations, and produce in their own good time what comes into their bird's brains.

It is touching to find that such affection for a parrot or a toucan or a goat or even for ants is not a one-way affair. Who can fathom the nature of such a relationship which somehow points to a closer and deeper community between the various species than we ordinarily assume? Is it unscientific to speak of the soul of a toucan, or shocking or ludicrous? Schweitzer once said, "This question of whether animals have a soul or not is difficult to settle. One thing is certain: in order to find out, you have to have one yourself!"

Human Imprints

One cannot describe a few hundred individuals. This is a pity, for every individual is unique and several hundred faces in Lambaréné have made their imprint on my memory.

As I see it, the word "man" has no plural. The concept "men" is one of our basic delusions. Every one of the remembered faces is "man" in the singular, and deserves a lifetime of attention. Given anything less, he is done inevitable injustice. Hence all description is partial in both meanings of the word: incomplete as well as prejudiced. I found people in Africa whose customs were very different from our own and who lacked most of the second-hand knowledge we pass for culture. But I did not find people basically more "primitive" than those who spend their lives running after the acquisition of more and more and newer things. The primitive is no longer confined to the bush, neither is the savage, who, I learned, is the person who feels that I-the-Subject has more reality, more right to live and express itself and to be without pain, than You-the-Object.

Could it be that this lack of insight in the relativity of I and You, their fundamental identity, is what Christian thought describes as "original sin" and Buddhist thought as "ignorance"? Hence, whether one is white and a doctor or black and a patient; whether one reads Vergil, Kierkegaard, or Mickey Spillane or whether one is illiterate, seems to me totally irrelevant.

Old Joseph, for instance, is neither a bookworm nor is he unsophisticated. He is thin and six feet tall. "I am as old as the Grand Docteur. I was his first assistant," he introduced himself proudly. He showed me the tooth that hurt, put his tall staff in the corner, and sat down in the chair. After the extraction he bowed with great dignity. "Thank you infinitely, *mon Docteur*."

He knows all the tricks of the most polished Western politeness. Originally a cook, he became Schweitzer's first orderly half a century ago. He still describes anatomy in terms of the menu: "He has a pain in his cutlet" or "a furuncle on his *bifteck*." He is given to philosophical remarks: "Sickness comes by plane and leaves on foot." He can talk as unctuously as a minister and once when I pointed at the local witch doctor and said, "Look, there goes my colleague," Joseph blinked the little eyes in his folded face and said, "Do not say that, *Docteur*, for you heal by the power of the Lord and he by the power of Satan and for money only."

Old Joseph never mentions that he left Schweitzer at a critical period during World War I, bought himself a number of wives, and went into the doctoring and lumber business for himself. Misfortune, however, followed on his heels. The wives either did not thrive or else they ran away, his doctor practice went wrong, and he found himself involved in endless semijuridical palavers. A few years before her death Emma Hausknecht found him in great misery in his village, forgave his defection, and brought him back to the Hospital. Leaning on his patriarchal staff with his exquisite manners and dignified bearing, Old Joseph gets a record number of presents from visitors. He sports a Fifth Avenue dressing gown and a fine wrist watch. He constantly complains that he is cold and underfed which is often true because Joseph is a great trader and likes to sell pullovers, blankets, or anything else that he receives.

"I would still be living in splendor," he confided to me, "if Emma had not kidnaped me and brought me back to the Hospital."

But then there is not only Old Joseph. There is Young Joseph. Compared with Old Joseph, the patriarch, he is young; he has only been an orderly for twenty-four years. He is a quiet man who does all the microscopic examinations and knows more about the eggs of tropical parasites than many a learned doctor. He has, however, throughout the years fulfilled all possible other functions

Old Joseph, Dr. Schweitzer's first orderly

at the Hospital. He can act as midwife, knows sterile techniques, is in charge of the distillation of water. On the day of my arrival he showed me all there was in the line of dental instruments and he knew about their uses. He was immediately interested in everything I did and in a few more months I could have made him into something like a very adequate emergency dentist. He also felt responsible for keeping my clinic spotless.

Joseph's upper and lower front teeth were missing. And although I did not have any dental laboratory equipment I managed to improvise an upper and lower partial

Young Joseph does all the microscopic work

denture for him, of which he was tremendously proud. It was shown to the whole population of Lambaréné. This resulted in a run on the clinic, for now everybody wanted such a magnificent apparatus. As for Joseph himself, it gave him the status of a person who all at once had come in possession of a country house and a Cadillac.

When I said good-bye Joseph had tears in his eyes, and as I stepped into my pirogue someone gave me the following note, scribbled by Joseph:

> We thank you infinitely, Monsieur le Docteur Franck, for the great service you rendered. As long as we are at the Hospital there has never been a dentist who has rendered us such great service. We wish you good health, good trip and . . . until next year,
>
> Joseph

This letter as many other communications, prescriptions, and bills at the Hospital bore the printed heading "Cognac Martell"! I never saw the connection.

Young Joseph had a little nephew, Darri, who became my assistant. That is, he cleaned and sterilized the instruments and swept my clinic with utter devotion. Within a day he could easily distinguish all the little drills and all the confusing little hooks a dentist pokes with. He must have been around thirteen. He came to the Hospital as a patient, suffering from a nearly fatal bone disease. The English doctor pulled him through, but both his arms remained withered. He could not do very much work for he could not lift anything heavy. Very intelligent and knowing eyes stood shining in his child's face. Over his spindly legs he wore frayed shorts. The hands on his mutilated arms were gentle and clever. I had been warned that he was a great sinner; once upon a time Darri had stolen a fish.

Moral codes at the Hospital are terribly strict. It is not only the Protestant hypertrophy of conscience and guilt feelings, but, as I found to my surprise, also native tribal pride is rigidly unforgiving. I never understood it, for the native's respect for property, I always heard, is rather relative. Yet Darri's uncle, Young Joseph, said, "I'll never forgive him. That a boy from my clan should be caught stealing is unheard of."

When Darri got sick one day, his family asserted that he was just lazy. The stigma cannot be washed off. I had to prove with a thermometer that Darri had a high fever.

He was very proud of his job with me and I photographed him in an orderly's apron, holding a piece of dental equipment in his hands. I hope that Reverence for Life may save this child who once was caught stealing a fish.

One of Darri's friends was Jean-Paul. He was twelve years old, rather tall, and it was some time before I discovered the seriousness behind his child's face. For as soon as he spotted me his whole face became one radiant smile of eyes, ears, and white teeth all laughing in unison. He was my guide on a trip to a little plantation a few miles up the Ogowe from the Hospital. I discovered that he had a deep tropical ulcer on his heel and took him to the Hospital to be treated. As soon as his ulcer got better he started to work, quite voluntarily. He would drag huge pitchers of water from the well to the rooms of the white patients. He carried heavy trays with dirty crockery back to the kitchen. He always spotted me from far away, and drew my eye with his sunniest of all smiles beamed from somewhere between the palm trees.

Jean-Paul was overjoyed with a little shawl I gave him, which he wore as a badge of honor. Next morning he came shyly to my room and brought me a pineapple.

When I was about to leave he and Darri Daniel sat all during the packing, on the porch in front of my room. They looked sad and seemed to be consoling each other. I believe these two were the last human beings I saw when finally the pirogue, taking me back to the airstrip, rounded the bend of the Ogowe which cuts the Hospital from view.

If Old Joseph embodies the World War I phase of the Schweitzer Hospital and Young Joseph the period between the wars, Jean-Claude is perhaps an embodiment of the new Africa.

Jean-Claude cannot be described by the semimilitary word "orderly" nor by "male nurse." Only the French equivalent *infirmier* seems to fit Jean-Claude. He is about twenty-three, slender and rather fair-skinned, with a keen, sensitive, almost feminine face. Is it perhaps this feminine element which makes him such an excellent comforter of the sick?

He lives now in a hut back of the Hospital with his young wife. The hut is unimaginably primitive. It has a clay floor and contains, apart from a calendar and a few empty tins and enamel basins, nothing but a rough bed and two native chairs. The young couple, however, show off proudly their neat home. Their manners are particularly civilized and courteous without servility.

Jean-Claude arrived at the Hospital on foot from very far away a few years ago. He had served a local doctor and had made up his mind that he would become an *infirmier*. When he heard about the Lambaréné Hospital he decided that his career had to start there.

He is too intelligent to be very popular with all the doctors and nurses. Everywhere in Africa there are still whites who prefer Africans to be a little stupid, subdued, and docile. Jean-Claude is none of these things, which is no longer exceptional. Many others among his young colleagues also have a quite correct appraisal of the white personnel with whom they work. I noticed that they sense exactly how good (or not so good) various doctors are. They have genuine respect not only for medical knowledge but especially for character. But they still have to bow to those who shout loudest.

The only characteristic trait of all the African staff is their extreme sensitivity to the psychological peculiarities of the whites on the staff. When the *infirmiers* are sure that nobody "dangerous" is around, they often give impersonations of white staff members which are not only devastatingly witty but betray an uncanny and even unnerving insight.

Dr. Catchpool considers Jean-Claude his favorite helper, devoted and intelligent, and feels that he can train him to become a most valuable, highly specialized, independent worker—if they both get the chance.

Jean-Claude asked me to take his photograph. He posed for it with a chest X-ray in his hand, holding it against the light. His eyes were concentrated on the X-ray, not on the camera.

Jean-Claude is representative of the new Africa we can lose or win. It just depends on how ignorant we are, how foolish or how intelligent.

Dr. Catchpool is thirty-two and looks forty. An English Quaker, he came to work at Lambaréné for six months and stayed two years. He was probably not fat when he came, but had lost an additional thirty-five pounds by the time I arrived, and his long hair, which was seldom combed, was prematurely gray.

Catchpool is very English, although he has nothing of the standardized public school product. He looks like a throwback to Gothic times, as though his father were one of those Saxon knights who, frozen into stone, lie on a sarcophagus in Ely Cathedral. He has none of the smugness or the prima donna complex which characterizes many doctors, in the jungle as well as in the city. Late at night followed by his dog, the Petroleum Mutt, with whom he has a violent love affair, he goes to his ward, looks at his plaster casts, sits and smokes with nearly every individual patient. He cracks little jokes in his private version of the French language. Later in his room he gets worried about a child deadly sick with meningitis, brought in that afternoon. He smokes incessantly as he grabs book after book to read up on meningitis. He is also an expert mechanic. One day he constructed a suction apparatus from a foot pedal of an old-fashioned dental engine, so that the child's mucus could be sucked out without switching on the large motor and waking up the Hospital. He also built the mobile bed for the paralytic in the New Ward.

He is a superior doctor, but entirely different from

most other doctors I have known insofar as no patient is a mere case to him. Even though he tries to hide it under the semblance of a stiff English upper lip, he shows in every gesture and movement his complete involvement, medical, human, and personal, with the humblest primitive human being brought in from the bush. I think he loses weight because he literally gives of his own substance instead of only from his professional training.

Dr. Catchpool is violent in his talk. For much at the Hospital, much in the attitudes of some other doctors, hurts him; all injustice or indifference seems to offend him personally. He is completely color blind, not even being able to distinguish black from white. He sometimes loses all sense of time, becoming totally absorbed in a child with breathing difficulties or a finger which has to be amputated. He really embodies the spirit of brotherliness and Reverence for Life with which the name of Schweitzer is identified. Should he ever, heaven forbid, read these words he certainly would throw a fit and mumble, "Utter bosh!"

Another aspect of total devotion is incarnated in Ali Silver. She is in her forties, but very young. She has the clear blue eyes and nobly cut face of a medieval Flemish saint in an altarpiece by Van der Weyden. She might also be a countess on a miniature by Corneille de Lyon.

Actually Ali has worked here for ten years without rest, except for one short vacation in Europe from which she could not return fast enough. She works like one possessed, and a catalogue of her tasks is impossible. Apart from being head nurse, she runs practically the whole administration of the Hospital. She is personally in charge of all white patients. She orders medicaments, bandages, instruments, and tries to keep her stock lists complete. Usually she also has a few animals as her special wards, perhaps a young antelope or a goat which would die without Ali.

In the mornings she assists at operations. She meets and organizes the "entertainment" of the many, often difficult, visitors. As a side line she scans innumerable newspapers for items which might interest her Chief and reads an endless number of often silly manuscripts sent to Schweitzer with requests for criticism, foreword, or recommendation. She wades through the contents of bags of mail reaching Lambaréné from all over the world, letters often intended to involve Schweitzer in various schemes, sometimes with dangerous political implications. She starts work at six in the morning and after everybody else's light is out, she is still answering letters, writing thank-you notes, politely declining applications from cranks. During meals she sits at Dr. Schweitzer's right and shares with Mathilde Kottmann the task of relieving him from having to entertain anyone who chooses to set foot in the Hospital and interfere with the workings of the staff, for no one is ever sent away or refused.

Dr. Schweitzer has three right hands—his own, Ali's, and Mathilde Kottmann's.

When, on arrival, you first notice Mademoiselle Mathilde from your pirogue you think, this is a lady. Coming closer, as she looks at you formally through light gray eyes from under her big sun helmet, you feel a little shy. The helmet makes her thin face old-fashioned and impersonally sahibian. You wonder, how shall I get on with her? As she courteously shows you to your bare little room, asks you to make all your wishes known, leads you around and with a discreet little movement of her hand points in the general direction of the "comfort station" called "Hinter Indien"—just in case of need— you think, Where have I seen her before? Was it in that elegant little pension in Munich? No. It was at the girl's *pensionnat* in Lausanne. The lady had offered you a chair in the bare rectangular reception room and had said with most correct sweetness, "Actually, you know, the visiting hours are from two to four, but. . . ."

At lunch, while Schweitzer ate his soup with leonine concentration, it was Mathilde who inquired kindly about the various hardships of the trip, the meteorological conditions between Brazzaville and Lambaréné, and other harmless and polite topics.

The lady Mathilde never disappears, but the woman Mathilde becomes clearer each day of your stay. She is Dr. Schweitzer's ever-present protector, who with great common sense tries to give him that minimum of rest which without her he would never get. She supervises the entire household of the Hospital, is its social secretary and hostess, its filing clerk and public relations director. She is also its peacemaker. She notices every one of the unavoidable small irritations and frictions in the community and makes certain that conflicts are solved before they become serious.

To contemporary taste she might seem too Victorian, too elaborately formal. Her efficiency is not of the I.B.M. type. It is impossible to imagine her somehow hooked up

Not an executive with five telephones

to a switchboard. But then, do not forget there is no switchboard here and Dr. Schweitzer is not an executive with five telephones, governing the smooth workings of a New York hospital.

Since she is so discreet and so wise, let me also be discreet and wise, just bowing deeply in the direction of Lambaréné, where Mademoiselle Mathilde is at this moment certainly doing something which in her considered opinion is helping the Hospital and saving Dr. Schweitzer from some unnecessary chore or worry.

Buru is Mademoiselle Mathilde's first assistant, in her function as the Hospital's postmistress. All those bags of mail arriving from every corner of the world and all the outgoing letters go through her hands. But it is Buru who paddles these loads to and from the Lambaréné post office in his pirogue. He also despatches telegrams. This is a complicated operation. An urgent telegram I tried to send to San Mateo, California, was first returned in order to find out whether San Mateo was a state, a second time with the question whether California was a city. The third day Buru returned with the postmaster's revelation that California indeed existed according to the Lambaréné telegraph office, but San Mateo definitely not.

Buru is an aristocrat; not just someone belonging to small rural nobility, but the descendant of a great family. Who else could allow himself such humble and exquisite courtesy? I once asked him to bring me some chocolates and cigarettes from Lambaréné-Downtown. "How much do I owe you, Buru?" I asked. He smiled my question away and waved his fine hands with such airiness that I could not possibly insist and had to accept his present as graciously as it was offered. I had even thought of tipping him but it is no doubt easier to tip a U.S. Senator.

The first time we met, I caught myself instinctively bowing to him. "Who is this man?" I asked the doctor to whom Buru had handed a letter. The doctor then told the following story. It may be true:

Many years ago the King of the Galwa tribe had his palace on the border of what now are the Hospital grounds. His people were highly cultivated and peaceful. Then the primitive, aggressive Fung tribe invaded the Galwa Kingdom. The Galwas were vanquished, eaten, or sold into slavery, all who could not get away across the Ogowe. The Fungs, being land people and afraid of water, did not pursue the Galwas beyond the river. The strong antagonism between Galwas and Fungs has survived to this day. Buru is supposed to be one of the last living grandsons of the last King of the Galwas.

Another remarkable personality is Muka.

Nobody knows how long Muka has lived at the Hospital. There are various estimates. Some people say "from before the war," without specifying which one. Some say "from just after the war," and they mean World War I. Muka sits on his bed in the New Ward. He is paralyzed from the waist down. His poor legs are drawn under him. His face would be called ugly by anyone who does not know what genuine beauty is. It is grooved by a thousand wrinkles and the protruding eyes look sadder than those of a sick dog. But look at him, smile in recognition, and his amazing face returns a smile of a million wrinkles.

He is the great friend of all the inhabitants of the New Ward. Children come and play with him and young sick·Africans sit in his cubicle playing checkers. Muka is always busy. He splits bamboo into the thin little sticks used for cotton applicators throughout the Hospital. One could not say that Muka works feverishly, but he works constantly. He takes time to look around and to smile at his visitors. He asks me—wordlessly, irresistibly—for some tobacco, looks out through the mosquito screening over the river, and turns back to check how many sticks his knife has meanwhile cut.

Apart from his professional activity Muka has his chickens. Usually two or three of them are sitting on his bed and a few walking around. Muka loves his chickens and since he has so much time to sit on his bed, he has developed the extraordinary skill of hatching their eggs himself. There must be some technical difficulties involved and some manufacturers of hatching machinery may deny that it is possible to replace their products by a paralyzed gentleman. But I take full responsibility: Muka hatches his chicken's eggs and produces Lambaréné's most beautiful chicks. He proves that, apart from one's main profession, one can have avocations which can keep one creatively occupied, handicaps notwithstanding.

I told Muka about a very dear friend in New York who is paralyzed exactly as he is. "He, too, works all

The extraordinary skill of hatching eggs

day," I told him, "and enjoys life. He does not cut bamboo sticks but writes books, and his friends love him also and come to talk to him." Muka seemed to think that writing books must be as entertaining as chipping bamboo.

"But he has not thought of keeping chickens yet. I'll write to him." Muka nodded a smiling assent.

"I like my chickens," he said, and grabbed one and started to stroke it.

Africans on the whole have no idea of their age. Ask a woman how old her children are and she makes four or five gestures with her hand to show their approximate height.

Papa Mathieu is different. He is blind and his fine Galwa features express nothing but wisdom and infinite benevolence. "How old are you, Papa Mathieu?" I asked him.

"Ninety years, six months, and seven days," he answered.

"And Cecile?"

"My wife is seventy-nine."

I wanted to check, for this was too fantastic in its precision. "When were you married?" I continued:

He thought a moment. "In eighteen ninety-seven," he said, "when Cecile was eighteen years old."

They sit hand in hand on their bunk, both utterly neat and clean. Papa Mathieu always wears a snow-white sleeping cap. His blind eyes now serve only to express his kindness.

"Have you any children?"

"We had many," answered Papa Mathieu in his pre-

cise, very cultured French. "But they are deceased," he
added (he did not say "dead"), "many years ago." He
translated into Galwa for Cecile who speaks little French
and she nodded resigned assent. His fine French can be
easily explained; in his younger years he had been inter-
preter for a governor.

I met Mathieu and Cecile when I started to draw him
one day while he was sitting alone on his bunk in the
ward. Cecile came, peered over my shoulder with her
nearly blind eyes, and said, "Instead of drawing him,
Docteur, why don't you operate on his poor eyes, so he
can see again?"

I did not understand her halting French and asked a
young patient to translate. Then I told her, "Nobody

Mathieu and Cecile

can operate on him, *Maman*, and give him back his sight. Your husband is very old. The nerves of his eyes cannot be repaired. Nobody can make you into a young girl again with a smooth face, can they, *Maman*?"

She looked at me gravely. I lifted my sun helmet and showed her how bald I am. "Who could operate on me and give me back my hair?" I asked. "Isn't that what life is like?" She nodded and understood.

We became great friends and nearly every day I visited a few minutes with Papa Mathieu and his wife, bringing them some tobacco. I would put the tobacco in his old hand and he would always say, "A little for me and a little more for Cecile, for she smokes more. I have my *bronchite* you know, Docteur." And Cecile would fill her short clay pipe and sit there smoking contentedly.

But Africa is not just Mathieu and Cecile, Jean-Paul, and Young Joseph. Africa is also Monsieur Okumé.

During a conference at the Protestant Mission, a few miles upstream, missionaries and their wives and children had gathered at Andende from all over the forest to discuss the rotation of their leaves to the motherland. The conference had barely started when the rickety old motorboat from Andende stopped at our landing, and from my window I saw some twelve men and women clamber on land, determinedly headed straight toward my clinic. Indeed a few minutes later about a dozen people were standing there sticking fingers into their mouths to point out teeth, gums, and abscesses in urgent need of treatment. What could I do but work until deep into the night at furious tempo?

All of the missionaries were white except one. His name was Monsieur Okumé. He looked shy and at the same time aggressive. He wore well-pressed trousers and a navy blue jacket in contrast to his white colleagues in their khaki pants and crumpled shirts. With a yellow leather brief case under his arm and a camera case dangling on his chest, he glowered at me through gold-rimmed glasses. Instinctively, I examined him among the first few patients. He refused to part with his brief case and camera, which actually hampered my movements. An immense amount of work had to be done for him, innumerable fillings and extractions. I juggled my overburdened schedule in order to accommodate him. I did all I could to make it clear that the white missionaries and the other patients had no shadow of priority. Monsieur Okumé came every day during the conference, and I worked overtime for him, but he would never give me so much as a smile of recognition. He only criticized what I did. He refused to stand in line for a few minutes with other patients in order to get a much needed shot of penicillin. He shouted orders at Joseph, the orderly who was helping me. He refused to follow any instructions whatsoever and when finally, on his last visit before his scheduled departure, I stood for two hours under the broiling operating light to try and complete his treatment it was he who complained about the heat of the light.

When it was all over Monsieur Okumé stalked out, camera case on his belly. I called him back, "Monsieur Okumé." He turned around. "I worked harder for you than for anybody else. You were not charged a penny. Can't you say 'thank you'?"

He looked at me with hate in his eyes but said, "I wanted to come back later and thank you."

Later, whenever I saw Africans in jackets, with brief cases and camera cases, full or empty, I was reminded of Monsieur Okumé. Yet I know that I am no reactionary, no white supremacist, not even unconsciously. Or is it perhaps that Westernization did something very wrong to the Monsieurs Okumé?

In contrast again to the "evolved" Okumé, there was my friend Emane Daniel, who looked more like the traditional "primitive." He was of the Fung tribe, lived in the Fung ward, and would not be caught dead with a Galwa. His occupation: fishing net mender.

Net mender

Noticing that I was drawing him he stared at me darkly and he even succeeded in making me feel a little uneasy. "You give me that picture (usually they say photo) when it is finished," he said threateningly.

"I can't," I lied, "it is for the Grand Docteur." This excellent excuse saved me much trouble.

Then we started to converse. The ice was broken and Emane and I became friends. He had some trouble with his legs and was unhappy about his treatment. When he came here first, years ago, he told me, they had given him injections "here"—and he pointed to his arm—and they had worked fine. But this time they wouldn't give him injections in his arm, but gave them in his behind and that did not do him any good. I went on drawing and Emane repeated the story a number of times for emphasis.

"Okay," I said at last. "I'll see to it that you get an injection in your arm." That afternoon Emane got an injection of Vitamin C in his arm, which by special dispensation of Providence brought great improvement to the whole list of diseases which I checked on his chart. Of course professional ethics prevent me from divulging the case history of Emane Daniel. Our friendship became very close and Emane, who always wore the colorful native toga, asked me for a shirt. I gave him a shirt and so we became bosom friends.

He confided in me and said he wanted to stay at the Hospital forever. In his village he had been poisoned twice. And he had neither mother nor sisters nor father nor wives nor girl friends, so why should he go back? If he got a little better he could fish for the Hospital and mend nets. I promised that I would take the matter up with the authorities and the authorities, of course, said that nobody was ever thrown out of the Hospital if he wanted to stay, and so I could reassure Emane of his tenure.

This poisoning story was quite typical. Africans, when they get sick, usually look for the poisoner or magician who brought on the disease. In every community there are certain people whom you are sure do not wish you well. Whether Emane had ever really been poisoned, I'll never know. In any case, the diagnoses on his charts could hardly be explained by chemical agents and suggested that although he might have been without father, mother, wives, or brothers, some girl friend must have sneaked in somewhere, somehow, sometime.

My relationship to Emane Daniel became closer all the time. He reported daily on his various aches and pains, *"cu-cu-cu-cu-cu-cu-cu,"* and pointed along his back or his legs. After the injection in his arm, of course, he felt much better.

He had therefore every right to write a letter to his distinguished friend which follows, carefully translated:

Monsieur le Docteur:

I have the honor to come with the greatest respect to join your High Benevolence. To tell you that you, who love me and I also who loves you, that is: let us be friends! I hope that when I shall have recovered, I shall remain your servant here at the Hospital. Pardon me a thousand times, because I hereby ask you for the sum of five hundred francs as a credit, which I shall return to you, when I have recovered. I live in dependence upon you. If you were not a doctor, I could not live. I have nothing more to say than to ask your forgiveness.

Please accept, *Monsieur le Docteur*, my respectful and devoted feelings.

Yours,
Emane Daniel

This letter touched me so much that without even sterilizing it I stuck it among the precious mementos of Lambaréné.

Entrances and Exits

$\mathcal{F}$or years and years the Hospital was completely isolated, its only link with the outer world being an irregularly arriving mail and an occasional visitor who braved long ocean voyages and uncomfortable river steamers to visit Dr. Schweitzer. There still is no telephone at the Hospital, but nowadays hardly a day passes without the arrival of one or more guests. Some of them are polite and ask beforehand whether they are welcome; some of them are less polite and just send a telegram, "I'm coming"; and many are downright rude and just stand there with one camera on their bellies for ordinary film and one on their backs for color, asking "Where can I find Doctor Schweitzer?"

Habits of hospitality at the Hospital have survived from the time of the Ogowe riverboat. Guests casually falling out of the sky a day after they leave New York are still received in the old courteous style. Courteous is an understatement, for the whole staff is often inconvenienced by a group of people who have no reason for coming here other than to be able to say at home that they have seen Dr. Schweitzer. On two occasions a group of culture-hungry matrons from a cruise ship were sent here to see the Hospital. For the travel agency this tropical slumming was no doubt an inexpensive extra entertainment. The thirty females were properly fed at Schweitzer's expense and the only dislocation they caused

The "powder room"

was that all the nurses had to sleep on improvised beds in order to accommodate them. Many of the ladies had never heard of Schweitzer until they started their trip and learned about the main attractions of Africa: Victoria Falls, Kruger National Park, the Pyramids, and Albert Schweitzer. The ladies were much impressed, though disappointed by the "powder room" where they had to queue up. During my stay a number of parasites of this kind arrived. For two or three days they were in everybody's way, had to be entertained, or perhaps I should say, contained, by one of the staff. They stood around snapping pictures of the lepers, who are very sensitive about having their pictures taken, criticized the hygienic conditions, and of course had to be photographed with Schweitzer before leaving.

One of the ladies, a "gorgeous blonde" in her fifties, had never read a word of Schweitzer. She was gaping at the dressing of leprous ulcers when I asked her about her impressions. She answered radiantly, "It is just out of this world. I am enjoying every minute of it!"

I have often suggested that the one apparatus most needed at Schweitzer's Hospital is an oversized catapult to shoot this kind of visitor back across the Ogowe to where they came from. But Dr. Schweitzer hates gadgets. He earnestly explained to me that he never refuses to see people because there is always a chance that one may reject exactly the one person who is in real need of help.

Not all visitors are of this species. During my stay a few physicians, very capable ones, came visiting, and their stay, even of a few days, was fruitful and stimulating to the doctors who have always problem cases to discuss.

Subtly, visitors are graded in order of importance. V.I.P.'s are received in style. When a plane load of French Air Force generals arrived, for instance, Dr. Schweitzer even dressed up. His dressing up is a fairly simple procedure. I happened to see it once. Dr. Schweitzer got up from his writing at the ringing of the big bell and put on his sun helmet. Walking out of his room, he bethought himself and came back. He opened a drawer overflowing with pieces of string, pencils, and erasers, stuck his hand into it, and with a skill based on years of training, drew out a small once-black bow tie neatly prefabricated on a clip. It did not look like the mass-produced ones you buy nowadays. It was probably a handforged clip, made by the blacksmith of Gunsbach many years ago. Schweitzer quickly clipped it on and felt dressed to meet his V.I.P.'s.

He walked down to the landing to receive the dignitaries. Since the pirogue carrying them was not yet close by, he took his little bag of rice out of his trouser pocket and fed the chickens along the path. There was the usual handshaking and the gentlemen were entertained at lunch. One of the party, perhaps an army chaplain, wearing a pince-nez, did what is seldom done at table: he got up and made a solemn speech in which he beseeched the Lord to spare Dr. Schweitzer for many more years in health and strength. Schweitzer listened politely and made a very short reply. He said, "Let us hope the Lord is listening."

On such occasions he has a twinkle in his eye which no professional snake charmer could improve on, and usually the twinkle is followed by a special wink which will disappear from this earth with Schweitzer.

Of course there are always missionaries passing through who use the Hospital as a hotel. Local authorities drop in for lunch and even the "Chief of Police" from Lambaréné occasionally sits down at table in the full glory of his uniform. On Sundays the district doctor, who is also director of the government hospital in Lambaréné-Downtown, traditionally comes to dinner. Cases are discussed and an informal atmosphere prevails. Dr. Schweitzer often is in a very good mood, reminisces and tells anecdotes which amuse him and everybody else. One of his most charming stories was a memory of his school days. One day as he was coming out of high school in Mulhouse, he saw people walking toward the railroad station with big bunches of flowers. "At the time," he said, "I was not quite as busy as I am now. The people with the flowers were talking English and I expected something was going on. So I followed them and when I got to the station a train with four carriages was just pulling in very slowly and Queen Victoria was looking out of the window just where I was standing. So I gazed long into her eyes. She looked very kind and motherly in her little black cap. She came from Nice. She always traveled by German railroads because the French trains went too fast for her taste. That was in 1889."

Visitors arrived every day at the Hospital, sometimes very boring ones, and although Schweitzer was always polite and hospitable, I often saw that this constant stream of chattering people exhausted him. But he was amused, as was everyone else, by a little man we nicknamed "St.

Francis," who dropped in for lunch one day. St. Francis was a puppeteer who went all over Africa for the love of God in Heaven, and to earn a living for his wife and six children in France. He was a little man of about forty, with a brown beard, big childlike eyes, an exalted manner, and an unending stream of rhetoric in which the word God was never separated by more than ten other words. He belonged, as he said, "to a Catholic society of lay missionaries, not too popular with the Church." He felt that the Church had something against him because he had this wife and six children, but God clearly wanted him to play puppets to the poor children of Africa, who unfortunately were terribly curious, pleading constantly to be allowed to look behind his apparatus to see how the puppets were worked, and had to be held off with a whip. But still, God wanted him to go on and he had his *camarade* with him who handled the money and played the puppets, while he held off the children. Besides he did not want to handle money because money corrupts. So his *camarade* handled it and sent some of it to the Saint's wife. He had just been thrown out of the Cameroons, had had typhoid four times, malaria seven times, dysentery fourteen times, had been in prison twelve times, but God wanted him to go on and spread His Glory throughout Africa. He felt much better now, for his children in Paris had made an important sacrifice: they did not eat chocolate any more, and ever since then God made his health improve, except that he fell from his bicycle and suffered a concussion of the brain. He would be very happy to give a performance for the patients whom God had punished with sickness, but since the overhead was so

high he would have to charge fifty dollars for his performance. The Catholic Mission school across the river
had already engaged him for this afternoon but he could
perhaps do it tomorrow for the Glory of God. By the
way, the Church probably did not like him because he
was not strong in dogma.

With the famous glint in his eye Schweitzer listened
to St. Francis until he heard the word dogma, at which he
interrupted the seemingly unending stream. "Forget
about dogma," he said, "except the dogma that you have
to take quinine every day or malaria will get you in the
end."

"Would you have time for an interview tonight, Dr.
Schweitzer?" asked St. Francis.

When Schweitzer heard the word interview he took
up his table knife and made a mock attack on his guest.
"Don't you dare to pronounce that word here," he said.

"Oh, excuse me," said St. Francis, "I did not mean to
interview you. I thought you might want to interview
me about my adventures for the Glory of God."

"Sorry, I'm too busy just now," Schweitzer said,
getting up, "but do come back for lunch tomorrow,
Monsieur." I heard him mutter to Mathilde, "I wish I had
that gift of gab!"

During the afternoon the Saint came to my clinic and
had a tooth out—free, of course. He also wangled a roll
of Kodak film and after blessing me went on his way
praising the Lord for my good anesthesia.

Every visitor and many non-visitors have appraised
Schweitzer. I don't feel I have to conform. Everybody
has from time immemorial appraised everybody else in

the style and according to norms fashionable at the moment. What is easier than a pompously psychoanalytical description or a sketch in the semantics of sociology? Contemporary essays and books about Albert Schweitzer neither add to nor diminish his stature. A man is not measurable, he just is. He is, whether his organ playing is approved or not, his Bach biography accepted or criticized, his theology current or superseded, his Hospital glorified or debunked.

The man who is, can merely be pointed at, and may reveal himself in little traits and unguarded words of small yet absolute significance. Often, I feel, his anecdotes are more revealing than his philosophy. Here is another one. The visitor was a young Ethiopian diplomat, just returning from a course at Harvard. At table Schweitzer asked him, "Have you any minerals in Ethiopia?"

"Not many," answered the dark young man. I translated his reply into German.

"Any gold?" Schweitzer insisted.

"No, sir, no gold," the young man said.

"Good for you," Schweitzer approved, "but how about oil?"

"Not as far as I know."

"Wonderful. Congratulations!" said Schweitzer. "You might be left in peace for a little while yet."

Later in the evening the young man went to bid good-bye to the Chief who was writing slowly in longhand under his kerosene lamp. I had to translate again. Schweitzer first gravely autographed the inevitably requested photograph. Then he wanted to jot down his

visitor's name and address. The Ethiopian handed him
his visiting card.

"Sorry," said the old man, "I can't give you one of
mine. I found I can get on without them."

He started to look in his address book. Like all his
other notebooks it is homemade of scratch paper held
together by bits of string. He thumbed it, mumbling,
"Algeria, Britain, Chile, Deutschland," but he did not
find Ethiopia. His eyebrows knitted, he started all over
again and found his Ethiopian friends listed under Abys-
sinia. Slowly he copied the address from the visiting card.

"Better have it correct," he said, peering over his
glasses. "You never know how you may need it one day.
For instance, if you become a refugee."

"What do you think, Herr Schweitzer, you might
become a refugee from?" I asked, laughing.

He looked at me gravely, but with a twinkle. "Who
knows, in our century, what he will be a refugee from,
or when?"

Schweitzer Without Halo

On the second day of my stay I told Dr. Schweitzer that I had been one of his listeners when he gave the Gifford Lectures at Edinburgh University in 1936. It seemed to please him. Three weeks later he mentioned something he had said during these lectures. "Don't you remember?" he said. "You should, after all you were there."

Some people say Schweitzer is a saint. This may well be. But since I have so little personal experience with saints I lack all competence on this question. I am sure, however, that his memory is an improvement on the electronic computer. He not only remembers word for

164

word lectures from his student days and innumerable
facts and anecdotes, he also—at eighty-four—remembers
a detail you mentioned casually in a conversation three
weeks previously. Whether it is in medicine or politics,
theology or music, metallurgy or pharmacology, if
Schweitzer knows a fact in any field he knows it precisely. If you talk about coffee cultures he'll ask, "Which
coffee?" and mention three botanical varieties. He will
then inform you where this variety originated and between which altitudes it will grow or not grow.

Before you open your mouth he has tripped you up.
Not pedantically, but simply not understanding that
other people's brains are a bit vaguer and less systematic
than his. Of course I remembered only very dimly what
he had said in Edinburgh in 1936 and I said so. "Actually
all I remember," I confessed, "is that your hair and your
mustache were still very black and that you were wearing a Prince Albert coat."

"Of course," said Schweitzer, "I always wear it on
official occasions. It is the most practical garment that has
ever been invented. As long as one knows," he added
with precision, "that in France it is worn unbuttoned
and in Germany it is very bad form not to button it. In
fact, at a reception many years ago Frau Hugo Stinnes,
wife of the great German industrialist, was very embarrassed that I was wearing my coat *à la française* and she
asked a mutual friend to tell me tactfully that I looked
very uncivilized."

"The Prince Albert is not worn very much any
more," I said casually.

"That is a pity," Schweitzer replied, "it is such a practical garment. I had mine made when I had to play the organ for the King of Spain in Barcelona."

"When was that?" I inquired. He thought a moment.

"In 1905, yes, 1905. Or was it in 1906? No, no, it was 1905. I remember it very well, for I said to my friend, the tailor in Gunsbach, 'You have to make me a frock coat for I have to play for the King of Spain.' He got very embarrassed. 'You mean to say, Albert, I have to make the frock coat you are going to play in for a king?' With a worried expression on his face he then said, 'All I can do is my best.' It really became a beautiful frock coat, very strongly built, and I have always worn it on all great occasions. Of course I haven't got it here, so I can't show it to you, for in Africa it is no use. I keep it in Gunsbach. But I wore it when I performed the marriage of Theodor Heuss, the present President of Western Germany, in the church of St. Nicholas in Strasbourg in 1907, when I was minister there. Of course I wore it, too, when I gave the lectures in Edinburgh, when I got the Goethe Prize, when I received the Nobel Prize, and when the Queen of England decorated me. And the last time Theodor Heuss saw it he said, 'My, my, Albert, don't you look elegant! You must have a very good tailor in Gunsbach.' "

Here I interrupted him. "You mean to say you are still wearing the same frock coat?"

"Of course," he glared at me, "that thing is still good for two hundred years."

To me this is the most typical story of Albert Schweitzer the man. When I saw him in 1949, coming up the gangplank of the *New Amsterdam* in his stiff black suit, battered hat on his head and peasantish umbrella over his arm, I thought, this man has cultivated a manner. He plays Albert Schweitzer all the time.

After you have seen the Grand Docteur at Lambaréné for two minutes, you know that he is not playing anything. He *is* Albert Schweitzer. The stiff black suit was probably constructed by his friend in Gunsbach around 1910. In Africa he wears a sun helmet, a pair of old but always clean khaki trousers, and a white shirt. Since the suit never wears out, why should one buy a new one? He is completely unaware of such trivialities. I have heard many opinions about Albert Schweitzer, some very devotional—and a bit embarrassing. More recently, especially among sophisticates who got tired of seeing him in the illustrated weeklies, the opinions were rather cynical: Schweitzer, the self-advertiser, the all-round genius who, they said, was above all a public relations genius; Schweitzer, the vain peacock.

There has been indeed a lot of publicity about Schweitzer, but certainly never consciously of his own making. With all his unparalleled gifts of heart and intellect he is often naïve about people. He is naïve in allowing himself to be exploited for the benefit of ambitious, frustrated society ladies. Earlier, he needed even their help, because he had to feed increasing numbers of indigenous and indigent patients. He had to build an ever-growing Hospital on grounds he had to buy. He was principally dependent on many modest gifts from all over the world. For long years he had only a relatively small but serious and faithful following, which supported his Hospital in as far as he could not do it himself by giving organ recitals in Europe. Only after the Nobel Prize and his visit to America was he discovered as "big news" by the world press and did he become fashionable. I am sure he cannot be swayed by playing on his vanity. But he can easily be exploited by anyone who succeeds in appealing to his strong sense of duty or to his ever-ready human sympathy and deep compassion.

"When I arrived in New York," he said, "and all those reporters were let loose on me, I felt like a virgin thrown to the lions in the arena. In the apartment where I was staying, one day a piano tuner came in and when he thought I was not looking he was taking photographs." So he was tricked and is still being tricked again and again into schemes not of his own making, without even realizing that he is being exploited. He is an easy touch, for he has unlimited confidence in the decency of people and hates to hurt, not only flies and other insects, but especially people who ask him for a favor. Some time ago he received a letter full of flattering phrases asking him to be the Honorary President of a Sports Festival in a small town in Germany. He replied that, as he was not a sportsman, he did not feel he should be the Honorary Patron, but he did not object to his name being included in the sponsoring committee. To his horror he discovered later that he was mentioned as a sponsor of a Communist Sports Festival for Peace in Warsaw.

It is certainly not Schweitzer's fault that the impression has been created that Africa between the Sahara and Johannesburg is a gigantic complex of savannah and jungle with somewhere in the middle the little jungle hospital of Dr. Schweitzer. As this synthetic legend has it, sick people and animals from all over Africa converge (to the accompaniment of tom-toms) on Lambaréné to be healed. This legend was no doubt created when a copy-hungry press found a new victim in the aging Doctor. During my stay a visitor, looking quite innocent but not innocent enough not to be diagnosed by me as a professional journalist and photographer, stayed for four days, was housed and fed—as everyone is who comes to Lambaréné—without any questions asked. Back in Europe I bought a French illustrated magazine of enormous circulation which contained a completely ridiculous account of the visit, including all the romantic clichés, and a few photographs, obviously tricked to make Lambaréné a great deal more jungly than it really is. Although the climate for months had been as pleasant as during a New York spring, this journalist saw perspiration dripping from all foreheads, had Schweitzer go for long walks along the Ogowe—where you can't walk for more than a hundred yards—and so on. The headline was: "They Had Crocodile for Dessert."

Pinkish journalists like to stress that Schweitzer talks of "natives" and so call him a reactionary. He may use old-fashioned terms and he may even be critical of the black people he has worked with for nearly half a century, but he has done them more good than all politicians and demagogues who use more contemporary terms. It is Albert Schweitzer who never left them and will work for them until his last breath.

I have even heard him called a fascist. This "fascist" during the thirties got a letter from a Nazi bigwig asking him for his adhesion to the noble Nazi cause, ending it

"*Mit Deutschem Grusz.*" Schweitzer wrote back that he declined the honor and signed it: "*Mit Zentralafrikanischem Grusz!*"

On the other hand, of course, he is accused by the extreme right of being a Communist. But then, who isn't?

His farm is his kingdom

To me Albert Schweitzer of Lambaréné is what in German is called a *"Groszbauer"* (great-peasant) and his Hospital is his farm. This kind of peasant is not just a farmer, he is a European phenomenon, a man rooted in his soil and living in a very special relationship to it. His farm is his kingdom; he rules over his farm hands and maids with paternal authority. In this sense Schweitzer is a *Groszbauer*.

This explains what has been labeled his "patriarchal tyranny," which is not a tyranny at all.

He is the owner of the farm who decides that the cowshed is going to be here, the new dung heap there, the horse stable on the other side of the yard. He does not just own his farm, he built it.

The Hospital was not just built by hired labor, and there was no architect to make the plans. The great-peasant said, "Here will be this ward, there will be that ward, here will be the cabins for the orderlies, there will be the Pharmacie. Good. Now we'll build the dining room on top of the hill and the guest house in the valley."

Over forty-five years, building continued on Schweitzer's domain. He was the architect, contractor, overseer, and, more often than not, foreman and laborer. I realized all this one night when I was ill and he visited me. To me my room was a cubicle, not particularly attractive although I had become attached to it. The Old Doctor probably had not seen it for a long time. He looked around with obvious satisfaction.

"Nice room, isn't it?" he said. He went over to the wall, looked at a diagonal beam and pushed against it. "Very strong," he said, "that can stand a tornado or two."

Then I realized suddenly that I was not lying in a room but in a creation. It had been built years ago with lumber and native labor and with Schweitzer's substance.

The household section of the Hospital is not African at all. It is like a *Bauernhof*, a West-European homestead somewhere along the French-German or Belgian-German border. The palms which grow there are actually a bit anomalous; they should be apple trees or poplars. The outhouse fits this farm better than would a white-tiled lavatory.

On the porch of Schweitzer's cabin a calendar is hanging. It bears appropriately the advertisement of a Strasbourg hardware firm.

Would an old *Groszbauer* listen to every newly arrived snippet who wants the dung heap moved a mile to the west and the stable changed into a den? Wouldn't he rather kick the fellow out? Would he think of ordering a hundred spools of string as long as there are drawers full of bits and pieces that you can tie together? Schweitzer has built his farm-hospital with his own hands. He has given to it more energy and perseverance than most of us possess. He has every right to say in his eighty-fourth year, "If you want to change it, wait until I'm dead."

I use the word peasant as a complimentary title. It is only in our mechanized age that it has become something of an approbrium. We prefer the agricultural engineer. But once it had a ring of nobility and the great independent peasant and landowner was a gentleman to be reckoned with. He was not a gentleman-farmer, he was a gentleman and a peasant. Schweitzer is not only a gentleman and a peasant. He is also one of the most versatile minds of our century. And not only that; he was born deep in the nineteenth century and is still here to demonstrate its greatness—and some of its limitations. As a doctor, and through his own initiative, he has brought solace and health to innumerable neglected sick people.

It is this great-peasant who presides at table, and if he shoves an extra piece of pineapple toward you, you must have deserved it. It is he who forbids one of the nurses to talk when she is eating fish. "You'll get a fishbone in your throat again!" It is the gentleman who will stand on the landing waiting for his guests as though he had nothing else to do. It is the peasant again who will not refuse hospitality to anyone who behaves more or less decently.

And it is with the shrewdness of a peasant that he sometimes answers questions. That is, when he is on his guard. The German-speaking editor of an American magazine of huge circulation was sitting next to me at table, opposite Schweitzer who, assisted by Mathilde, was being the perfect host.

"Did you have a good trip?"

"Oh, it was a very hectic trip," said the big man, "I was in Dakar the day before yesterday, then I had to fly to Brazzaville, this morning I flew in here, tomorrow I am going on to Johannesburg. It is pretty exhausting. By the way, Dr. Schweitzer, what is your opinion about national independence for the Africans of this region? Are they mature enough?"

Schweitzer slowly swallowed his spoonful of soup. He closed one eye and smiled a bit. "Well, you see, I am a lucky man. In the first place, I am just doctoring in my Hospital while you have to fly from Dakar to Brazzaville, from there to Lambaréné just to see me, and then on to Johannesburg. And, moreover, I don't have to interview and I don't have to have an opinion. You, poor fellow, do."

Very much more could be said about Schweitzer's over-life-sized peasant character. This incredible peasant is also the village cantor with a natural affinity to that other cantor Johann Sebastian Bach. Who has ever heard, however, of a cantor who at the same time also functions as teacher, pastor, organ builder, and doctor? And Schweitzer does not just function on a mere village level but has succeeded in lifting all these capacities to world significance. The cantor became the celebrated organist and Bach biographer, the teacher developed into the creator of the philosophy of Reverence for Life, the pastor became the authoritative theologian, the organ builder wrote a standard work on the subject, and the doctor grew into a universal symbol of human brotherhood.

The crucial fact about Albert Schweitzer, and that which makes his long life into a profound message to every man, is that in the face of all obstacles a man succeeded so absolutely in developing everyone of his potentialities to its utmost limit.

Au Revoir, Lambaréné

The day came when I had to leave Lambaréné. The three bells were ringing and the people who had become my friends streamed to the beach where the pirogue was waiting. Patients and doctors, black people and white.

It had seemed an adventure when this pirogue had brought me in from the airstrip some months ago. Now Lambaréné had become part of my life and leaving seemed unreal, even impossible. Obiange the chief oarsman, pushed off. The people on the beach were already receding. They were all waving. Schweitzer was standing in front and shouted, "*Auf Wiedersehen!*" Mathilde's smile was still visible. Ali was waving something like a sweater. In the water Darri and Jean-Paul were wading after my dugout. Then came the inevitable bend in the Ogowe and the people and the Hospital disappeared.

In the plane to Brazzaville the other life suddenly became real again. In my mind I already heard the chatter at my next New York cocktail party.

"Tell me," I heard, "tell me all about it."

"How is it really? Isn't it wonderful, wonderful to be with such a wonderful, wonderful man?"

"The Hospital is indescribably dirty, isn't it, and medically completely obsolete? And of course he really never was a doctor at heart . . . he is essentially a theologian. . . ."

"Yes, but isn't he in the first place a great philosopher?"

"Philosopher? Not at all. I know what I'm talking about, after all I teach philosophy, and I can assure you. . . ."

"I have *all* his organ records. Isn't he a marvelous organist?"

"He is quite a decent organist but his musicianship. . . ."

"And what about his biography of Bach?"

"Well, at the time he wrote it there was very little literature on Bach, you know."

"I think he is one of the world's greatest scientists, don't you?"

"Now come on, Jean. He may know a thing or two about tropical diseases but since when does that make you a scientist?"

"You know, I believe it is all a racket. A big publicity

stunt. There must be a lot of money in it. After all the whole world. . . ."

"No, no, he is just a vain old man. He just makes pronouncements on everything. Now, it happens to be atomic energy."

"It is interesting, isn't it, but people just have to have a mythological Father figure."

"Of course, don't forget he is also the only so-called saint of whom the Protestants can boast."

"His attitude toward the Africans isn't just colonial, it's pre-colonial."

"Oh, but I love him. I think he is a wonderful, wonderful man!"

"Of course, there are clearly elements of self-punishment, Christian guilt feelings, you might say. . . ."

The shadow of the plane sweeps over the endless patch of cabbage called a virgin forest.

What is the Grand Docteur doing now? He walks from his room to the Pharmacie, feeds his chickens, looks in at the operating room, has to greet two nuns who came to see a doctor, sits down and starts to write, still has to figure out a tax return. He works, bent over his little table, consulting scraps of paper. Later he'll put on his helmet and climb the steps to the dining room and eat his soup. If he is lucky there are no visitors. Then he'll go on working until suppertime. He'll play his prelude and read his Bible. He'll tell a joke, go back to his room, study a few phrases of an organ work, and then sit there answering the thousands of letters. He'll look through the press clippings, deeply worried about the drift to collective suicide. He is not worried about himself at eighty-four and in Lambaréné. He'll go on writing till deep into the night. Then the heavy old body will stretch out on the iron bed under the mosquito netting.

May he awaken tomorrow, look out over his farm and Hospital, his animals and his trees, and exclaim again, *"Ist es nicht wunderschön?"*

"Is it not wonderful?"

Au revoir!

Afterword

Lambaréné Revisited

The following account of Frederick Franck's return to Lambaréné, some years after the experiences recounted in My Days with Albert Schweitzer, *is reprinted from Franck's book* African Sketchbook.

It was pleasant to leave Douala and fly through an overcast sky to the Gabon Republic. In the plane I set next to a gray-haired African with a finely cut face, who was correcting a manuscript. He addressed me in especially elegant French. "Are you going to visit our newly independent country?" he asked, slightly ironically, "in which case I bet you are going to Dr. Schweitzer." He was the editor of a local newspaper, a patriot and a conservative, which made him a friend of Mr. Leon M'Ba, Prime Minister of the new republic. "During the independence celebrations," the editor told me, "M'Ba made a speech which was a model of moderation. He was educated in France like myself, and for years he was a deputy in the French Parliament. The Premier sees very well that the Gabon needs France. As long as Mr. M'Ba is premier here, the Gabon will be a cultivated country, but," he added with a worried look, "elections are coming, and if the demagogues win we might get into a Congo-like situation. Then I would not vouch for the safety of your friend Schweitzer either."

"What do you think of Schweitzer?" I asked. "Oh, I admire the man," he replied, "I realize very well that without Schweitzer few people would ever have heard about our country. He has done tremendous good here. But the young hotheads hate him and that is understandable too, for they can't realize Schweitzer has been here for nearly fifty years and that when I was a child he was about the only doctor in the whole country. They only see that there are now modern hospitals here and there and that the Schweitzer hospital is becoming an antique."

At the Libreville airport *buvette* they were drinking beer. The blond woman behind the counter was shouting instructions to the kitchen. A black boy, shining like a new shoe, brought in a large *capitaine* fish for Friday lunch.

The next stop was Port Gentil. The customs officer with his heavy, kind black face recognized me. He had been my patient at Lambaréné last year and asked me for a prescription for pills to improve his potency. At the mouth of the Ogowe River lies Port Gentil—an enormous sky of pearly gray, a strip of beach with a few high palms, a sleepy street parallel to the beach with new ugly houses built by the Petroleum Company. There is not a ripple on the polished mirror of the bay. Not a soul stirs in the Sunday streets except one man in a battered felt Homburg, who walks his dog. He looks as if he were walking in Valenciennes and had forgotten to put on his winter coat.

Here in the air-conditioned, gleaming new hotel I waited for my plane connection to Lambaréné. Since the country has become independent it has its own airline, which consists only of a few planes chartered from Air France and hence the number of flights has been greatly reduced. But to rest two days in this pleasant atmosphere of indolence is no punishment. Main Street has a few bookshops with the newest French literature. Is this turbulent Africa? All the Africans speak French, and waiters and postal workers talk to you like equals, quite naturally and with dignity. How far away is humming Lagos, terrorist-infested Douala, and seething ex-Belgian Congo? *Ici tout est calme et beauté.* . . .

Lambaréné from the air: a homecoming. The plane again noses its way over the green jungle soup with its patches of island and comes down on the airstrip, where they are now building a smart control tower. At the Ogowe River ferry, the large pirogue from the hospital is waiting and the rowers Emile and Obiange and *petit* Jean welcome me like a lost brother. The river is very low in the middle of the dry season and on the large sand flats fishermen are camping in palm-leaf huts. Little black boys are playing a game, sliding off the high river banks into the turbid water. The same crews on the same old steamers are still coming and going and we recognize each other. A boy in a pirogue shouts, *"Bonjour, Docteur!"*

At the hospital landing there are more pirogues than ever. Dr. Schweitzer has aged. He is building again, a row of new huts for his workers near the new garage. He looks worried and drawn, completely wrapped up in his building. "I still have to build this," he says. "When I am dead they can get on for a few years yet, but then there will be nobody here who can organize this." It was the first time I had heard him mention anything about the hospital after his death. I am constantly asked about Dr. Schweitzer's plans for his hospital and usually answer: "Can you predict what will happen in Africa next week? How can anyone make plans?"

The hospital has not changed. There are two new doctors and a few new monkeys. The young pelican has become an adult and a tame member of the family, and the velvety litter of off-white kittens of last year is now a family of mangy cats. Main Street is still choked with the sick, the shouts of *"Brancardier, brancardier!"* still sound from the beach when new emergencies arrive in canoes. I think I hear a woman singing from a pirogue midstream. The pirogue comes closer and what I thought was a song is a heart-rending wail. As the pirogue touches the beach the woman jumps out holding a child in her arms. The child's head dangles passively as the mother runs on her thin strong legs to the hospital.

Yet, also in Lambaréné things change. In the Leper Village a radio blares; it was given by a visitor. First I hear music, then a demagogue from Leopoldville speaks. Something has changed in the mood here too, and since Nurse Trudy left the children have forgotten their songs.

The old man was sitting at his table, writing. His head, bent low over his note paper, nearly rested on the table. He muttered something, started to rummage in his papers, could not find what he was looking for, and muttered louder. His housekeeper-nurse-secretary,

Mathilde, must have heard him, for she appeared in the doorway looking at the mess on the desk. Her hands folded she asked softly, "Were you looking for something, *Docteur?*" "Did I call you? Then stay where you are," growled the old man. Mathilde left meekly and Schweitzer went on digging in his papers. Then he got up, angrily. The old massive torso bent, the legs a bit curved in the frayed khaki trousers, the square bushy head thrust forward. He started to leaf through the clusters of clippings, bundled together with string, hanging from nails behind his desk. He was still mumbling, found what he wanted, and lowered himself onto the hard square stool ("I don't like chairs, I despise comfort"). He licked his fingers and leafed through the file of clippings.

Then he started to write again. His face was even closer to the paper now, a face built around a central massif core; the large pitted nose as its base and the heavy brow-arch as its top. From it radiated innumerable lines deepening into grooves which divided the aged flesh into planes; above his glasses the bushy eyebrows were knitting and unknitting, hairs sprouting and jumping over the rims. The line of the eyebrows was repeated two or three times in parallel grooves on his forehead. The skin looked hard, old, and element-beaten. The white mustache bristled over his mouth and nearly caressed the paper.

The old strong hand slowly, deliberately wrote on. Then after a sentence or two his head would straighten and turn. For a few seconds it would be fixed toward the glassless window with its mosquito screening and look out over the river. Suddenly he seemed to notice me again. "Shall I pose for you?" he asked kindly. "Oh, no, please go on working, I'll sketch you while you work." "Yes, but not with my glasses," he said, "they make me look too old." Within a minute he had forgotten me and was writing again. It was getting dark and the cicada music had become as strong and irritating as a blaring radio. The file of ants marching across his table got out of focus in the growing dusk.

When he pulled the oil lamp toward him and lighted it, I noticed for the first time that he was wearing cotton sleevelets over his wrists so that the sweat would not soil his paper. After a few more sentences he got up again. He took the sleevelets off and put on a faded crumpled felt hat. "Let's sit down outside," he said.

I followed him out of the room and we sat on the steps of his porch, looking at the dusk deepening over the river. He seemed sad about something he had just read. "One should have the skin of a hippo," he said abruptly and without explanation, "and the soul of an angel." His dog Tshutshu sat between us. Mathilde came noiselessly behind us, standing erect with the toucan Jackie on her shoulder, who was peering at us from the beads on both sides of his ludicrous beak.

The old man looked at the evening and absorbed it. "Look at that tree," he said, pointing at a kapok in the distance. It still was caressed by the last light of day. We stayed, silent, a few minutes longer. The darkness had fallen quickly like a hood over the landscape. The dinner gong was sounding and kerosene lanterns started their dance to the dining room. "*Ja, ja,*" sighed the old man. He got up heavily, took his kerosene lamp from the shelf, and we all crossed the yard to the dining room. We put our burning lamps to wait for us in the little hall.

The twenty people in the dining room, who had been talking, became quiet and sat down. The last chair stopped scraping on the conrete floor. Schweitzer's eyes quickly darted up and down the long table, then they closed.

"Thank the Lord, for He is kind and His goodness is everlasting. Amen," he said quietly.

During dinner I told him about a class of a public school in a poor section of the Bronx, where I had given a talk some time ago. The children, all thirty of them, had written letters to Dr. Schweitzer. "I just thanked them in your name," I said, "I guess that is all right." But the old doctor wanted to know all about it and I read to him some of the names—Spanish, Italian, Jewish, Polish, Chinese—and told him about the teacher who made it her task to teach all these white, pink, yellow, and black children to get on together, he looked at me with suddenly very young eyes under the bushy white eyebrows. "But this is important," he cried, "this is really important."

After dinner he asked me to his room and I watched him write with his old hands slowly and steadily two letters, one to the children of P.S. 53 in the Bronx and one to the teacher:

> . . . I myself come from an old Alsatian family of schoolmasters. My grandfather, his four brothers and two sisters were schoolmasters. And I, deep down in my heart, am a schoolmaster and have a schoolmaster's soul. That is why I undestand so well your work in the difficult and very special profession of a teacher. . . .

He is more than a great man, I thought, he is a great human being.

While I was drawing the next day, an African joined me. He was fortyish, thin and intense. It was clear he wanted to ask me for something. It was money. Then he started to complain bitterly about the hospital. He said he was working on the new road and hardly got paid. "Just because my wife is sick, I have to work like a slave," he snarled. "And the *Grand Docteur* insults us when he gets mad at us. You don't do that any more to us blacks. If he were a younger man, I'd bash his head in."

Even Lambaréné is changing. The "winds of change" which sweep all over Africa are not stopped by any wall of mahogany and okoumé trees. Schweitzer is still the great witch doctor to the old, but the young *évolués* dislike the hospital. It may have been true twenty years ago that the Africans were afraid of a gleaming white hospital and preferred one which reminded them of their villages. Schweitzer has often said so and his hospital did become a cross between an Alsatian farm and a native African village.

But the young Africans have a new god. Not the Christian one, whom they never really accepted— Christianity is losing in Africa, Islam is gaining—but the cruel god Progress. In Lagos I saw Yoruba women who lived in slums without plumbing or any sanitation proudly push the buttons of the self-service elevator in their new skyscraper hospital. No condescending pseudo-villages for them, but the shiny gadgets, the roaring power of car, plane, bus, and tractor, which at last will make them equals of the whites.

"Why is there no sanitary water in that hospital?" the bus driver asked me, blinking through his sunglasses. His hands were behind his khaki back and his chin was thrust up aggressively. He is the man who drives his bus from Lambaréné to Libreville and back once a week. "Why didn't the Grand Docteur ever start a school to train black nurses? Why are there still those dirty old bunks and no beds? Why does he separate the Fang and the Galwa patients? That was O.K. fifty years ago but we are all Gabonais now, aren't we? Come on, *Docteur*, have you ever seen the hospital at Libreville?" The bus driver knows what he is talking about. The hospital at Libreville, five hours by bus, is hypermodern and built in the latest international style. It is huge and no doubt excellent. "All of Gabon has only about fifty doctors, and look how this old hospital is filled day after day with three hundred and fifty patients or more," I answer. "How can you doubt it is useful?"

But the chauffeur is the New Africa and his quarrel with the Lambaréné hospital is not based on reason but on emotion. "*C'est dégoutant*," he repeats. And he will repeat it at all the bus stops between Lambaréné and Libreville.

On this third trip to Lambaréné my heart grew heavier and heavier. In America Schweitzer is criticized because the press took hold of him and exploited this news item until it became an irritant. His imbecilic adorers still pretend that his hospital is the only hospital in Africa, the only medical center on the tropical continent to which all the little Africans come running to have their ulcers cured with potassium permanganate; as if there were no hospitals and doctors all over Africa, albeit too few; as if there were no World Health Organization. Hysterical females sing his praise in falsetto and pour their adulation over women's club audiences, making a career out of eulogizing the old doctor, until those who never did anything creative in their lives feel justified in dismissing this great human being as a phony.

Meanwhile the old man plods on. Somewhere deep inside he must know that, although he was the pioneer of medical help in Equatorial Africa, he has been overtaken. He must, with his probing intelligence and his real love of human beings, feel deeply unhappy that he has under-estimated the Africans surrounding him. But even there I defend him, and have defended him against attacks all over the West Coast of Africa. For all the African doctors and intellectuals attacked me on Schweitzer, whom they see as a vestige of colonialism, paternalism, and a Christian endeavor they don't understand and hence despise. "He may be the noblest flower of colonialism, he is typical of the era," they say. They seem to decry the old curative hospital, which even if it is not modern and not perfect, has relieved suffering for nearly half a century. They think only in terms of the mass approach of preventive medicine. Meanwhile many African doctors, who are so quick to criticize the old pioneer, themselves flock to the cities, where almost all of them work for status, money, large houses, and gleaming cars.

Schweitzer has never been in Africa, I have often argued. After his short European "vacations," during which he gave talks or organ concerts to raise money for his hospital, he took the boat from Bordeaux to Port Gentil and from there the slow *pinasse* to Lambaréné, where he buried himself in work among a poverty-ridden, backward agricultural people. The more developed countries of West Africa he has never seen, and who of us a few years ago knew what went on in Accra, Abidjan, Lomé, or Yaounde? Who knows now? Meanwhile the Grand Docteur worked and cured and wrote and played his piano-organ and the years flew by, and the inroads of education and culture in his poverty-stricken district were far from spectacular. If he had come from his native Alsace to some forlorn hillbilly village in the Ozarks and never left it except by air, would he have a high estimate of American culture from direct observation?

My intellectual African friends often understood this argument, but my anxiety remained. If there were only hope of modernizing Lambaréné in time! But how can we expect Dr. Schweitzer at eighty-six to adapt himself to the mutations of Africa? Even if he were to install electricity and water and a school for nurses—even if he were to streamline his hospital out of recognition, banish his animals to kraals, import African doctors (from where?), who would guarantee that it would be sufficient?

One day Schweitzer must die, and the loss of this great human soul, this gigantic example of what a man can do with his life, will leave us all much poorer.

He asked me with something at once hopeful and hopeless in his eyes, "Do you believe that the idea of Reverence for Life is gaining ground?" Reverence for Life. . . . I came from New York and had traveled all over exploding West Africa, across half of a globe which seemed to be getting ready to destroy itself in a last general spasm of insane violence. Timidly I said, "I don't know. There has never been so much violence. And yet, you sowed a seed. . . ."

We were standing at the bend of the new road Schweitzer is building. After forty-seven years he has given in: the hospital will be accessible by car and truck instead of by canoe only. A yellow bulldozer was flattening the underbrush and the African driver was singing. The old man bent down stiffly and lifted a few much too heavy rocks. He put them carefully by the side of the road and mumbled: "I can use them for building later."